The Pastor's Guide *to* Growing *a* Christlike Church

George Hunter III, Kennon L. Callahan, William Willimon,
Stan Toler, Jerry Brecheisen, James Earl Massey, Mary Paul,
H. B. London Jr., Neil B. Wiseman, Adam Hamilton,
Robert Leslie Holmes, Ron Blake, Darius Salter, Tom Theriault

Beacon Hill Press of Kansas City
Kansas City, Missouri

Contents

❦

Introduction

The Body of Christ, the Community of Faith, the Fellowship of Believers—these are only a few of the images associated with the Church. Taken together they all refer to something quite different from any club, institution, or business. Here is a people drawn from all peoples, infused with spiritual life, and called to a great mission.

Such vitality and purpose belong to the Church wherever it is. Unlike any other organization, the local church is not a separate part of the whole; it is the local expression of the whole. Yet each local church needs a guiding hand—a pastoral hand—to help it flesh out what it means to be the Church.

This is not an easy task. As a pastor you are tugged in so many directions to "do church" in so many different ways. One technique promises larger offerings; another, better attendance. Responsibilities, denominational and otherwise, pull and stretch at how you do your job. It's hard to keep focused. Sometimes the pastoral vision of nurturing a community to reflect Christ's vibrancy, purpose, and love gets a little hazy. Even worse—you must sharpen this vision and accomplish this nurture in a world saturated in consumerism and postmodern uncertainty. Where can you find help amid so many distractions and complications?

This book seeks to provide some of this help. In the following pages experienced church leaders recapture and refine the vision of what the Church is and what its task should be. These leaders serve in diverse capacities. Several are educators; some are pastors; all are seasoned ministers. In these chapters they share their insights in such areas as leadership, worship, renewal, fellowship, outreach, and missions. They explore their topics with an eye on how the local church can be made a clearer reflection of what it truly is—*the* Church.

Take some time and allow these mentors to refresh, inspire, and guide you. You won't be disappointed, and you may go away with a better idea of what great potential your congregation has. After all, to its neighbors your church is the Body of Christ. Let God use this book in your ministry to help your church encompass all that this means. Not only will your people and their mission be enhanced, but almost certainly you will be too.

William Willimon, S.T.D., has been dean of the Chapel and professor of Christian ministry at Duke University in Durham, North Carolina, since 1984. He has served as pastor of churches in Georgia and South Carolina. In 1996, an international survey conducted by Baylor University named him one of the Twelve Most Effective Preachers in the English-speaking world. He is the author of 50 books. His articles have appeared in many publications, including *The Christian Ministry, Worship,* and *Christianity Today.* His *Pulpit Resource* is used each week by over 8,000 pastors in the U.S.A., Canada, and Australia. He serves on the editorial boards of *The Christian Century, The Christian Ministry, Pulpit Digest, Preaching, The Wittenburg Door,* and *Leadership.* He has given lectures and taught courses at many pastors' schools, colleges, and universities in the United States, Canada, Europe, and Asia. He is married to Patricia Parker. The Willimons have two children: William Parker and Harriet Patricia.

Building a Spiritual Church

William Willimon

❧ PAUL'S FAVORITE TERM FOR THE CHURCH IS "THE BODY OF CHRIST." That is a high calling. Paul claims nothing less than that the church, your church, my church, is the physical form that Jesus takes in this world. When I think of my church (and yours!) that may seem to be too exulted a designation. When one encounters the grubby sociological reality of the church, as opposed to the exulted theological designation of the church, well, it can be quite disillusioning. Nevertheless, for better or for worse, your church and mine is the physical form that the Risen Christ has chosen to take in the world. The church is the flesh of the Word made flesh. If people are to encounter Christ, it will be through the church or nothing else.

Life in the Body is tough. John says that "the Word became flesh" (John 1:14) in Jesus Christ. Keeping the transcendent Word and the immanent flesh together in the church—that's hard. In my experience we pastors tend to get caught up so much in the mundane, fleshly, institutional, and organizational duties associated with caring for the Body —raising money, going to meetings, keeping the roof from leaking, refereeing in congregational squabbles—that it is all too easy to lose sight that this Body is nothing less than the Body of *Christ*.

All rites of ordination are clear in asserting that the primary vocation of pastors is to be those Christians who are set apart for the maintenance, care, and correction of the community. We are, in our ordination, distinctly "community persons." We pastors are set apart for the specific vocation of caring for the Body, working for consensus in the congregation, nurturing the visibility of the church, preserving the church from one generation to the next. It may be enough for individual Christians to nurture and nourish their own little spiritual garden. As for pastors, we must worry about those matters that keep the community the community of Christ, that keep the individual members in communion with one another, and that keep us with Christ. It is all too easy to allow our ministry to degenerate into mere administrative maintenance of the Body—as if the church were just another helpful community organization among many other helpful human organizations—without continually pointing the Body toward its high theological vocation to be the Body *of Christ*.

There is this constant tendency in the church, particularly among those of us who are called to care for the institution of the church, for church to degenerate into becoming just another human organization, a civic club with a religious tinting, a group of like-minded people with a thin religious veneer. How do we keep refurbishing and rejuvenating the church as a peculiarly *spiritual* Body?

Years ago, when mainline Protestant denominations began to lose members, sociologist of religion Dean Kelley published his important book *Why Conservative Churches Are Growing*.[1]

Kelley's book was the first of an avalanche of studies on mainline Protestant church decline and Evangelical church resurgence. Among other things, Kelley claimed that the younger Evangelical churches were growing because they stressed strict doctrine, strong, even authoritarian pastoral leadership, high commitment, and other factors that were thought to be part of conservative faith. Kelley was widely praised or condemned for this view, depending on the particular church allegiance of the critic. But these factors were not at the heart of Kelley's argument. Kelley's main thesis was that growing Evangelical churches grow because *they stick to business*. What is the main business of the church? Kelley put it something like this—the main business of the church is to keep referring people toward God; to keep viewing the world under God; to keep putting the God question on the table; to keep asking, in all of its thought and life together, "What does this have to do with God?" Kelley claimed that churches grow when they never lose sight of this basic business of the church. Churches decline when they forget "It's about God."

A succession of studies has expanded upon Kelley's thesis. In their book on mainline liberal Protestantism, Kirk Hadaway and David A. Roozen say that when all factors related to church growth and decline are studied, "The key issue for churches seems to be a compelling *religious character . . .* , not whether the content of that character is liberal or conservative."[2]

These sociologists of religion claim that mainline liberal Protestantism is in difficulty because its churches have given people a theological rationale for godlessness. It is not, as some thought in the early '60s, that mainline liberal Protestant churches are losing members to more conservative Evangelical churches. Rather, the situation, according to these astute observers, is that mainline liberal Protestantism is losing people to the church. Mainline liberal Protestantism becomes the last stop for many people on their way out of the church. Or as one of my friends put it, "Many of our people woke up one Sunday morning and just couldn't think of a compelling reason to go to church. The church had become so much like the world, why bother?"

In a more recent book by Hadaway, _Behold I Do a New Thing, Transforming Communities of Faith_, he asks, "What is a religious institution?" He answers this question by asserting, "Religious institutions are those that connect or relate the everyday world, the immanent world, into a reality that is behind, beyond, or subsumes our world into the transcendent."[3] This may seem to be a too-fuzzy definition of a church, but it certainly demonstrates Hadaway's contention that mainline liberal Protestant churches have not taken care of business. Hadaway believes that churches have got to ask themselves, "What are we for?"

What unchurched people are looking for is the same thing that everyone expects the church to be; a religious organization. It should look different, it should feel different, and it should sound different, because unlike every other organization in society its specialty is religion (rather than something else—group fun, golf, scuba diving, bowling, good books, etc.). After interviewing hundreds of people in the United States and Canada that don't go to church, I have concluded that the predominant view of the church is this: It is not a particularly enjoyable group with a restricted view of morality and spirituality. Unchurched North Americans don't feel they need the church for social involvement, they don't think the church has a monopoly on truth, and they don't think the church would help them very much in their relationship with God.[4]

It is so easy for us pastors to become sidetracked in our leadership of the church. In our internal maintenance of the Body, we lose sight of what the Body is meant to be, how this Body is different from other bodies.

When I was a young theology professor, roaming about on the weekends among churches of my denomination, doing workshops on various topics of church life, I was surprised in my conversations with laity in many congregations to hear a frequent refrain: _We wish our pastor could be more of a spiritual leader._

"Spiritual leader"—what is that? In probing the laity on this matter, I heard them complain that their pastor had become little more than a manager of a volunteer organization. One layperson told me, "You can talk with our pastor about everything but God." Another said, "We asked our pastor to lead us in a Bible study, and he said he didn't have time with all the other demands of running a big church. What are pastors for?"

I expect these pastors would have been genuinely surprised to hear such a complaint from their laity. Yet the complaint is evidence that we have not been taking care of the unique business of the church.

As I consider many of the sermons I hear (and many of the sermons that I preach!), I hear a decidedly "a-theistic" tendency. I hear many sermons that are essentially on "self-help." In too many churches that pride themselves on reaching out to "seekers" and the "unchurched," I hear sermons that are little different from the advice one could receive from any self-help book. I fear that these preachers have allowed the seekers and their limitations to determine the content of the message. We Americans are a do-it-yourself society, a people who generally believe that if our lives are going to be better, it is mainly left up to us to improve them. We no longer want salvation, or conversion; we want self-improvement. Jesus becomes another helpful technique, among many techniques, for getting what I want out of life. Jesus becomes another "lifestyle choice" that helps me feel a bit better about myself.

The other day, watching "Dr. Phil" on the television, I at first marveled why anyone would want to put themselves through the rather excruciating critique of their lives that is offered by Dr. Phil. I heard Dr. Phil, the TV therapeutic guru, tell people such things as, "You must be getting something out of your sickness, or you wouldn't stay sick." Or, "You say that you want to change your life, but you don't. This suggests to me that you are lying and really don't want to change."

Why would anybody willingly expose himself or herself on television to this kind of ridicule? And then I realized that Dr. Phil is really flattering us and appealing to our cherished images of ourselves. When there is no longer a God who hears and acts, it is up to us to set our lives right, or our lives won't be right. We don't need to pray when it is all left up to us. We have got to take matters in hand, honestly diagnose our situation, pull up our bootstraps, and move forward—on our own.

I hear too many sermons that appear to be more indebted to Dr. Phil than to Scripture. These sermons say they are based on "biblical principles" or "spiritual rules for better living," but in reality they are advocating a form of self-help and self-salvation. Christians don't believe in self-help. We believe we cannot help ourselves, exclusively by ourselves. We need a God who saves, who reaches in, intrudes, and acts to do for us what we cannot do for ourselves.

(When you think about it, "self-help" books are a lie. We really can't help ourselves by ourselves. If we could, why do we have to spend $19.95 for a book by someone like Dr. Phil telling us how to help ourselves!)

Too many of us pastors have taken our models from essentially secular images of effectiveness. We are the skillful church administrator—electronic notebook in hand, moving efficiently from meeting to meeting, getting the job done, setting goals, reaching those goals, evaluating, improving, with purpose and direction. Or we are the therapeutic leader—helping sick people get better, offering people psychologically based techniques for self-improvement, enrolling them in therapeutic groups where the group is supposed to be their salvation. Either way, there is too little of God in these approaches to ministry. God sometimes offers us "biblical principles" from Scripture, but not God himself.

How can we keep our congregations close to the business at hand? How can we keep nourishing a sense of our churches as the Body of Christ, as essentially spiritual organizations that keep raising the God question and who keep turning our lives toward God? I have some suggestions:

1. Scripture

In the church's weekly rhythm of worship, in our constant encounter with the Word of God and its encounter with us, we keep being reminded of who we are meant to be. The pastor's task is, on a weekly basis, to lay the biblical story over our life together, to let that story become the lens (John Calvin) through which we read the world. Christians differ from Buddhists mainly in that we have listened to different stories. These stories teach us how to attend to our lives, tell us what is really going on in the world, where we are all headed, who is in charge, who we are called to be.

I work on the interpretative principle, when reading and interpreting Scripture for teaching and preaching, that the Scriptures always and everywhere speak primarily about God and only secondarily or derivatively do they ever speak about us. Scripture is an ever-present reminder that *it's about God*.

Leaving home for a meeting the other night, passing through my living room full of graduate students who had gathered at my wife's weekly disciple Bible study group, I said to them, "It strikes me that what you are doing is very odd, very strange. That a group of early 21st-century North American people should gather, open up this ancient book, written in languages so different from our own, in a culture so different from our own, and study that book word-for-word, verse-by-verse, with such care and attentiveness, with such respect and submissiveness, that's odd." I congratulated them for so attuning their lives to this holy text.

Then one of the group asked me, as I was on my way out the door for my meeting, "Is where you are going also odd, distinctive, and holy?"

The question sort of ruined my meeting! Yet it is precisely the question that more of us ought to ask in our round of church meetings. Is this meeting an opportunity for a true "meeting" with God?

2. Personal Devotion

The pastor helps the congregation be encountered by the Word of God in Scripture, by the pastor constantly being encountered by this Scripture. When I moved from the parish ministry into campus ministry, for the first time practicing ministry in an institutional context other than the local church, I found that I desperately needed to begin each day with an intentional, directed time of focus. This meant Scripture reading, not for the purposes of sermon preparation, but for the purpose of remembrance, refocus, and nurturance of identity. It also meant prayer—an earnest, intentional attempt to lay myself open to the claims of God upon the day before me. This time of meditation, before I began any other work, helped remind me of who I was, helped to focus my activity, caught my attention. It was a way of saying to me, "You are not a second-level academic administrator. You are a priest. Now go out of this office and look for what God is doing on this campus today and get with it."

I realized that my parish ministry would have been much more effective and faithful if I had taken this time of focus and reflection seriously when I was a parish pastor. How many pastors allow themselves to become distracted? They begin their day opening mail, answering the phone, caught up in the busyness of the pragmatic, the utilitarian, and the everyday. Or they get on that treadmill of running about, visiting at the hospital, counseling the troubled, caring for others when what they most need is a time to focus.

I've learned much from my work with military chaplains. Here are men and women in ministry in an institutional setting—the armed forces—that in no way has as its goal anything that can be called "Christian." What are they doing there? As one chaplain put it to me,

"When I get up in the morning, put on that military uniform, with military insignia and a cross on the uniform, all mixed together, I have to take a moment, look at myself in the mirror, and ask, 'What is my real mission today?' Is it keeping order in the army, keeping the troops pacified and docile, or is it service to Jesus Christ?"

The chaplains, at least the best of them, had learned that they were in a highly ambiguous, potentially dangerous (at least dangerous to their souls) situation that required reflection, focus, analysis, and care in how they went about their tasks, in how they defined their tasks, in how they used their time and for what purposes.

I believe those of us in more traditional forms of ministry would do well to spend some time in similar reflection as we begin our day, asking ourselves, "What about the work that I do today will be specifically, undeniably *spiritual* and not merely useful and helpful?"

I remember hearing Henri Nouwen say, "If you pastors don't know the absolutely essential, then you will do the merely important. And because so much of what you do is potentially important, you are apt to allow the important to crowd out the absolutely essential."

3. Corporate Worship

Marva J. Dawn provocatively titles one of her most recent books on worship A Royal "Waste of Time": The Splendor of Worshiping God and Being the Church of the Word. She is, in her title, pointing to the peculiarity of Christian worship in a utilitarian, pragmatic society that judges every person, experience, and institution on the sole basis of, "What will this do for me?"

We pastors ought to nurture among ourselves a strange view of being "effective." Much of the trouble starts when we try to be "effective." We measure effectiveness as the world judges these matters; we run about with such purpose and efficiency that one day you won't be able to tell the difference between a preacher and a politician, between a spiritual leader and a secular therapist.

I remember a Duke undergraduate bragging to me about her "great pastor" who had called her at midnight the night before, "just to talk." "He calls me about every couple of weeks," she said, "just to check on me. He is the perfect pastor. Always late to everything. Missed a wedding last summer! His car is always a mess, loaded with books and papers. He takes time for you. His lead question, in almost any conversation, is 'What's God doing with you now?' Really a great pastor."

And I marveled at the influence of this unorganized, sloppy, God-centered pastor on this upwardly mobile, driven, ambitious undergraduate student. I think that pastor constantly created room for her to be with God, for her to worship. We pastors need to stop asking so much "How can I be more effective?" and ask more theological questions such as, "What is God up to today?" "Where is God leading us now?"

Pastors are often criticized for "wasting time." But we must keep relearning the odd view we have of time. The church really believes that our most important business, our best use of time, is when we (in the world's eyes) "waste" time in the praise of God. In fact, think of Sunday morning worship as constant training in the attentiveness, the peculiar use of time, and the topsy-turvy value system of the Body of Christ.

My last congregation had many problems. They had lost hundreds of members in the previous decade. So much needed to be done when I arrived there. It was overwhelming. What did this church most need from me as their new pastor? How could I possibly get all the work done? In desperation, at the Pastor-Parish Relations Committee meeting, the committee that relates most directly to the pastor and the work, I gave the committee a set of 3 x 5 cards, each card listing a different pastoral activity—visitation, answering the telephone, visiting the sick, preparing sermons, and so forth. I told them, "This is your church. You may know more about what I need to be doing here than I, as your new pastor. I'm going to leave the room, and I want you to arrange these duties in the order of their greatest importance."

I left the room. They were in heated debate for the better part of an hour. When I returned to the room, there were all the cards, arranged in the order of priority. What was the number one, most absolutely important priority? Preaching. Number two? Bible study. Number three? Worship preparation.

Worship is that time in the week when we take time for God, when God takes time for us. An important priority for any church that would take care of business, that would be more spiritual, is the necessity to take back time, to redeem our time as God's time. Worship is training in taking back time.[5]

We must keep being nourished by the miracle of corporate worship: "And day by day, attending the temple together and breaking bread in their homes, they partook of food with glad and generous hearts, praising God and having favor with all the people. And the Lord added to their number day by day those who were being saved" (Acts 2:46-47, RSV).

4. Prayer

So much of prayer is a matter of paying attention, listening, helping God to make room in our world. Prayer is essentially how God speaks to us, not so much how we talk to God. Yet for God to get to us, we must be available to God. There is that tendency, particularly among the most conscientious pastors, to be busy, to fill up all the empty space with activity. Prayer keeps making room. Prayer forces us into that threatening silence, where we are no longer speaking or listening to others speak, no longer anxious about next week's sermon or tomorrow's Bible study session but rather where we dare to be silent and allow God to speak.

There is often too much pastoral chatter in our Sunday morning worship, where the pastor offers a running commentary, microphone in hand, as if we are the "color commentator" at a football game broadcast. Silence on Sunday, in worship, can be oddly threatening. I think it is a threat because in the silence, God can come.

So those of us who think of ourselves primarily as preachers, as speakers, may need, in order to develop a more spiritual church, to think more of ourselves as courageous nurturers of silence, creators of room that allows God to have God's way with the church.

Hadaway and Roozen say that when all factors related to church growth and decline are studied, "The key issue for churches seems to be a compelling _religious character_ . . . not whether the content of that character is liberal or conservative."[6] Dean Kelley was right in insisting that it is not so much that conservative churches are growing because they are theologically conservative, it is rather that they stick to the business of providing a theological rationale for people's lives. They keep focusing on God. Or as Hadaway and Roozen say explicitly, "To grow and to continue growing, a mainstream church must be a vital _religious_ institution, vibrant for the presence of God. It must have a clear _religious_ identity, a compelling _religious_ purpose, and coherent sense of direction that arises from that identity and purpose."[7]

I think it would be helpful if we pastors conceive of everything that we do as a form of prayer, of constant attentiveness to God, of constant expectancy for the intrusion of God, as a possible invitation to worship. Karl Barth says repeatedly in his _Church Dogmatics_ that theology is best thought of as prayer: an earnest attempt to listen to God. So in response to the question, "How can I have a more spiritual church?" perhaps the best response is to say, "Well, _you_ can't." A spiritual church, the Body of Christ, is something that God does. So we rephrase the question: How can God have a more spiritual church? How can Christ have a livelier, faithful body? I think the answer lies in part in our willingness to listen, to be open, to make room, and to dare to let Christ use us to be the Body that He deserves.

Notes

1. Dean Kelley, *Why Conservative Churches Are Growing* (New York: Harper & Row, 1977).

2. C. Kirk Hadaway and David A. Roozen, *Rerouting the Protestant Mainstream: Sources of Growth and Opportunities for Change* (Nashville: Abingdon Press, 1995), 69.

3. C. Kirk Hadaway, *Behold I Do a New Thing: Transforming Communities of Faith* (Cleveland: Pilgrim Press, 2001), 18.

4. Ibid., 39.

5. When Thomas G. Long studied a group of vibrant churches, and then listed the characteristics of their worship life that were significant, among all the characteristics he listed, the very first is that in their worship they "make room, somewhere in worship, for the experience of mystery." Long says, "Worship is about awe, not strategy" (Thomas G. Long, *Beyond the Worship Wars: Building Vital and Faithful Worship* [Washington, D.C.: Alban Inst., 2001], 30-31). In worship the church and its leaders make room for and take time for the most important act of business by the church—the glorification and enjoyment of God.

6. Hadaway and Roozen, *Rerouting the Protestant Mainstream*, 69.

7. Ibid., 86.

James Earl Massey is dean emeritus and distinguished professor-at-large at Anderson University School of Theology in Anderson, Indiana. For 50 years, Dr. Massey has been an extraordinary preacher, teacher, and communicator of the gospel. He served as the senior pastor of the Metropolitan Church, Detroit, Michigan (1954-76); the campus minister of Anderson University, Anderson, Indiana (1969-77); a speaker on the "Christian Brotherhood Hour" radio broadcast (1977-82); dean of the Chapel of Tuskegee University, Tuskegee, Alabama (1984-90); and preacher-in-residence of Park Place Church of God, Anderson, Indiana (1994-95). He has preached and lectured at more than a hundred colleges, universities, and seminaries in the United States and on four continents. He is a life trustee of Asbury Theological Seminary and sits on the editorial boards of *Christianity Today, Leadership, Preaching,* and *The New Interpreter's Bible.* His published works include *The Responsible Pulpit* and *Designing the Sermon. Sharing Heaven's Music,* a collection of essays written by his colleagues in honor of Dr. Massey, is also available.

2

Developing a Visionary Church That Has Integrity
The Cornerstone of Our Dream for the New Century
James Earl Massey

❦ THE CHURCH BEGAN UNDER A LEADER WITH THE HIGHEST INTEGRITY: Jesus of Nazareth, a teaching preacher. Intent on developing an effective working group for ministry in the world, Christ fashioned a community that looked to God, trusted His judgment, and had eyes of vision for claiming the world. Our Lord planned the church intentionally based on truth. He founded the church in order to have a community with integrity to continue His work in the world when He went back to be with His Father.

The Christian minister must always remember how the church began. He or she must know what the purpose for the church was in the mind and heart of the Founder so that we can follow the same lines of integrity by which Jesus established the Church. In our contemporary American setting, I am wary of the business model as the best image for the pastor because it smacks of commercialism and capitalism. The Bible's focus is on the church as a fellowship, a family, and a functioning community. And the pastor leads such a functioning fellowship built on integrity and energized by truth.

JESUS DEVELOPED VISION BY TEACHING TRUTH
I said that the Church began under the ministry of an itinerant teaching preacher. The emphasis on teaching was very strong in His ministry because He knew that those who came to hear Him needed truth—truth about God, truth about life. And He shared that truth

19

with them. In fact, so filled was He with truth and so fully shared He the truth that He came to be known as the Truth, as well as the Way and the Light. In His teaching, His major method for developing this community, He was masterful and so engaging that those who heard Him gladly called Him Rabbi, my master. He taught truth.

Again and again in the Gospel accounts, when persons were addressing Jesus in the midst of His teaching, they referred to Him as Rabbi or Teacher. According to the account in the Gospel of Matthew, the crowds were astonished at His teaching. It might very well be that in our day, teaching does not seem to have the kind of allure, the kind of attractiveness, that we read about in the New Testament on the part of Jesus. But when the Church began, it began around the central figure of a teacher of truth.

NEW TESTAMENT LEADERS FOLLOWED THE PATTERN OF JESUS

The New Testament writings reflect the fact that this spirit of teaching was not only in Jesus, who founded the Church, but also at work in the life of those who continued His ministry when He went to be with God. This spirit of teaching was strong in the churches during the first century for two reasons. First, Jesus as the founder of the Church had been a teacher come from God, and this kept the teaching ministry in continuing esteem. Second, the church leaders Jesus appointed to continue His ministry knew that sound living, or living with integrity, depends upon sound teaching.

John Knox, who taught for many years at Union Theological Seminary in New York City, wrote a special essay many years ago for a volume titled *The Ministry in Historical Perspective*, one of three volumes published in order to highlight theological education. In this specialized article Knox commented, "The fact that Jesus is characteristically known as a teacher must reflect not only the original fact but also, in some degree, the importance of the teacher's role in primitive Christianity."

The early teachers of the Church planned strategically. They intended to guide the awakened intellect, to provide religious answers for the questioning mind, and to offer a systematized body of truth for the questing soul. The teaching reflected and reported in the New Testament writings mainly involved believers—yes, persons already won to the faith through the preaching of the gospel. But the Epistles also show that what is taught was necessary as follow-up to what is proclaimed. The soundest basis for church growth is not merely to proclaim but to teach. Teaching the full implication of the proclamation helps to develop a church that has integrity.

By the time the pastorals were written, it was expected that those who chose to be pastors would be able teachers (1 Tim. 3:2). In fact, the stipulations regarding pastoral ministry made teaching an imperative function. Henry Sloan Coffin, who was the dean at Union Theological Seminary at the time John Knox was teaching, said, "A preacher who would minister in the same pulpit for a quarter of a century, or at least for a decade, and would train a congregation in conviction and ideals, in methods of intercourse with the Unseen, and in ways of serving the commonwealth, must follow a similar educational system as was followed by the Apostles."

In the New Testament, teaching is highlighted far more acutely than leadership. Then authentic leadership was provided the church through teaching the truth about God and life.

Given the unique history and posture of American society, no professional role has been more strategic to social progress than that of the teacher. And I would think that our society is in great disarray in our time largely because the teaching profession has been undermined.

This has also affected what happens in our churches. Teaching is not always valued. The founding and continuing development of the nation's churches, together with their strategic impact upon the development of the character of the nation during this several hundred years' experience and experiment in democracy, has depended in great measure upon the work of ministers who could teach. But we are, I fear, weakening or altogether deserting our ministry of teaching.

VISIONARY LEADERS ARE TRUST OFFICERS OF TRUTH

As a servant leader in the church, the minister shares status and authority with many others who are called and commissioned to be trust officers in the service of the Lord. We are called and commissioned to share and pass on the charismatic message about salvation and to train believers in the values and implementation of this good news from God. You and I as ministers are expected to teach what the church has always taught. In this service, we must follow the lead of the first Christian preachers and teachers, whom Albert Outler aptly described as "traditioners, trust officers of the Christian treasure of truth, qualified judges of right teaching."

As ministers, leaders of churches, you and I not only identify the tradition of which we are a part, but we are identified with it and by it.

When you and I stand to serve, we are standing and serving as trust officers who share the truth.

We are passing on something that is not novel or new. It is something that was here earlier. It was established by our Lord, and it must continue with integrity. Teaching is one of the strongest ways by which that integrity is passed on by way of concept and identification.

The Christian gospel is God's invitation to an experience, an experience inclusive of moral effects, spiritual effects, and social effects.

In our New Testament, we find the initial record of that experience as it is registered in the lives of distinct persons whose memory we hallow and whose names we continue to honor. But that biblical record is also the sourcebook for the kind of noble, serious, instructive, and necessary work that we must do as teachers. It is from within this province of the distinct biblical record that the Christian minister is expected and authorized to teach what the church teaches.

VISIONARY LEADERS ARE SHAPERS OF COMMUNITY

Along with teaching, pastors are expected to inspire and promote what generates social uplift and human advancement through freedom, justice, fairness, and the steady pursuit of community, which has been lost. Very little notion of the values of community are being rightly espoused in our time. We are privatized now in America. We are tribalized. We are competing. If this loss is to be turned back, it must be turned back by those of us who understand why the tradition was established and what it is intended to do in succeeding generations.

I don't know whether or not you view yourself as a teacher, but if you want to have a church that has integrity, it will have to come and be maintained by the method our founder used—teaching. Linked by calling and tradition to the event in the message of Jesus Christ, we are expected to be servants of God's Word to the world, teaching what the church teaches.

We are sharers in that grand and great succession of those who have dared to proclaim the Christian faith, those who have dared to interpret the Christian faith, and those who are seeking to fulfill the implications of the Christian faith. And you and I are linked by life and experience with people who are struggling to survive, who are trying to achieve in a secularistic and otherwise problematic society; and the best tool we can give to people in order to struggle well and aptly is truth, which is communicated through teaching. By teaching truth, we apply the insights of the faith and encourage people, uplift people, and guide people, after we have won people.

A church that has integrity must begin at the point of someone taught about the meaning of salvation. The church is the community of the saved. How are they saved? Through hearing the message of truth from the preacher. It is interesting how much Paul linked salvation with the messenger that brings the news regarding it. It is a truth handled, taught, shared, lived, advocated, modeled—integrity. Developing a church that has integrity by means of experienced truth must be at the core of our concern.

THE VISIONARY IMPACT OF PREACHING

First among the strategic means for this teaching that I am holding to your view again, is the ministry of preaching. Preaching rightly understood allows moral and spiritual instruction to be shared in mass fashion. It allows truth to be shared in a popular medium, but always with an individual impact.

According to the Synoptic Gospels, there was a blend between preaching and teaching in the ministry of Jesus. (There are passages in the Gospels in which the terms "preaching" and "teaching" are used interchangeably so that the action of Jesus in addressing His hearers in public appears pointedly didactic and declarative at one and the same time. As you review the Sermon on the Mount as told by Matthew and then by Luke [which is much shorter], you see the blend of teaching and preaching in the Master's life.) Jesus instructed in order to inspire. He gave content in order to share comfort. He declared at the same time that He explained.

Understanding is always imperative for those who seek to live out their faith, and aptness in relating biblical truth with personal questions and the needs of people keep the teaching minister linked with them as an essential helper of their faith.

This accent on teaching is part of the pastor's role, as I indicated from 1 Tim. 3:2, which requires the pastor to be an able teacher. This was highlighted in the first century, and the church grew by leaps and bounds. It must return to our concern if our churches are to grow by leaps and bounds with integrity. This readiness and skill to instruct must be reflected when the congregation gathers to worship God. It must be there when they are addressed out of God's Word—teaching through preaching.

True religious experience is more than an emotional mood. Today there is a great deal of entertainment in the midst of our worship. People view the excitement of the occasion as a clue to the vital happening, but unless something is being taught and caught, the integrity is missing.

THE VISIONARY EFFECT OF DOCTRINE

The climate of modernity does not inspire faith, although it does press persons to seek and locate a faith. Preaching in mass fashion calls attention to the Christian faith, and it does so by isolating certain facts and certain truths from inside the experience of that faith. So preaching that is religiously instructive must address matters of doctrine. Charles Spurgeon once said, "The most fervent revivalism will wear itself out in mere smoke if it is not maintained by the fuel of teaching." Sound teaching precedes sound living.

The concern to share doctrine must be a part of our passion—not doctrine for doctrine's sake, but for the sake of the people's understanding and for the use of faith by which to live rightfully. Doctrine is best focused when the way it can help has been understood first by the preacher. It then breeds life and imparts a liveliness. It shows itself in more than an abstract subject, and it claims attention as a necessary message that attracts, alerts, and assures. The earnest preacher will seek to make the most correct statement of the truth with which he or she is dealing, the most correct statement with which we are dealing at the time. But that statement must be pertinent to the needs of those who are to hear it. To merely preach doctrine is not enough. We must understand the implications of the doctrine for the lives of our people. This is the way integrity is developed in a congregation.

Biblical doctrines matter for life at its best. When somebody says, "I don't want any doctrine," they do not understand the importance of shared truth. Doctrines rightly understood, rightly shared, satisfy the soul's quest for truth, and they liberate the mind by engaging the thoughts. What a marvelous thing to leave the sanctuary at the close of a worship service and for someone to say to you, "I've got something to wrestle with this week because of what you shared this morning." The preaching that really matters does not separate inspiration from something that has been taught.

Howard Thurman used to tell about how impressed his grandmother was with the preaching that she, a former slave, had heard from a certain slave minister when she was a girl. The slave preacher was allowed to come to the plantation and preach about four times a year, and on each occasion he had drilled into the consciousness of all of his hearers the notion that they did not have to feel inferior because they were slaves. As Thurman used to tell it, everything in him quivered with the pulsing tremor of raw energy when in his grandmother's recital, she would come to the triumphant climax of the slave minister's message because he always ended the message the same way. "You," he would say, with his eyes fastened upon them, standing his full height, six feet tall— "You are not niggers. You are not slaves. You are God's children."

That kind of sharing of truth gave a people a grounds for personal dignity. Preaching that does not involve the sharing of truth at the level of human need is not what brings the church integrity. It is out of that profound sense of being children of God that the slaves could handle the pressures of their days. The idea that they were children of God was not something that the slave masters shared with them. They were sub- jects and chattel to the slave owners, but the preacher gave them that bedrock truth that brought them through. That is the foundation of the African-American faith. We must call the church back to this kind of level of understanding of who we are because of God's mercy and God's grace. We must share it.

The white preacher who served the master's interest always taught them, "Slaves, obey your master." That was the bulk of the training for slaves that the slave master's preacher sought to convey. He argued his doctrine defensively, intent to keep the people submissive. But the slave preacher applied his doctrine in the interest of his hearers. He sat where they sat. He felt what they felt. And he was intent to liberate their spir- its. That is the true function of sound teaching: to liberate people. You shall know the truth, and the truth shall make you free.

THE VISIONARY IMPACT OF PASTORAL CARE

Pastoral counseling ranks among the central services a minister is expected to make available to those who seek it. We teach by counsel- ing. Our effectiveness in counseling will depend upon many factors, of course, but the ability and the readiness to share insights and perspec- tives in dealing with persons who need help cannot be overemphasized.

Wayne Oates, one of the great and grand traditionalists of his pro- fession but also a great human spirit touched by God, listed several lev- els within the field of pastoral care, and one of those levels is that of teaching. As interpreters of the Scriptures and as ordained servants of the church, you and I must share perspectives that are of an instruction- al value, in spite of all the other theorists who insist that we cannot go about it that way. The necessity to instruct seems very clear when deal- ing with persons whose moral views are problematic, whose religious views are heretical, whose attitudes are unhealthy, and whose experi- ences need some clarifying conversation. It calls for instruction on our part as we counsel.

This religious care of troubled persons in our time must include the need to share information and insight, as well as a caring presence. The minister's counsel will be given to share insights, rehearse meanings, answer questions, resolve conflicts, appeal to motives, heal inward injuries, stimulate faith, purge the soul, promote change, provide emotional release, encourage persons to venture, and grant them enablement by which to move ahead on their own. Rightly done, the counsel that you and I share by means of our teaching can clarify life for the counselee and help the person to handle the confusion that experiences often bring. All of us can think of persons who have come to us, so direly confused that even we hardly knew where to begin in seeking to help them. When the counsel is instructive, inspirational, and supportive, it helps to center a person in order to make a wise and informed decision and to act in a way that counts. This is what I mean by integrity.

In the light of the minister's need to serve such ends and to serve them well, sound training for this kind of work is a must. Most seminaries rightly require ministers to prepare themselves for this through courses in pastoral care and counseling. Quite beyond the notion of counseling, there must be an understanding of truth by which to counsel properly.

THE VISIONARY IMPACT OF GUIDED STUDY

Another way by which we can help our church develop integrity is to teach a class in the church program. Given this teaching responsibility that devolves upon the trained minister who pastors, and given the investment of years of study in this ministerial role, it is not too much to expect the pastor to view the congregation as a school in Christian living and labor. The congregation comes to school whenever we are having worship. The congregation comes to school whenever we are studying in a formal way. And when that happens, the pastor ought to have a very special up-front role in the teaching process. Passing this off to someone else does not help a congregation to coalesce around its leaders.

I know some of you regularly teach a pastor's class that involves new converts, new members, young people, or children. This approach is fine, but it is better to engage the entire congregation in guided study if you can, either to examine a biblical theme or some biblical book or some issue in life from a biblical perspective with the minister as the teaching elder. I do not think the Presbyterians have it wrong at that point. They highly emphasize that teaching role of the pastor. But whether we do this with the whole congregation or within a small group from the congregation, this face-to-face approach as an involved teacher of the people permits a sense of partnership in learning, a sense of togetherness in being under the authority of the Word of God.

Adolf Schlatter, great German theologian of another day, had delivered a great sermon, in the eyes of a person who greeted him after the service was over, and she said, "Sir, I'm glad to meet a theologian who stands on the Word of God."

He said, "I understand what you mean, but I want to correct you at one point. I do not stand on the Word of God, I stand under it." When the pastor does this sort of teaching, the congregation is reminded that integrity comes by being under the Word of God.

This fundamental work of the minister in the congregation of believers is to share the Christian faith, interpret its significance for all of life, and develop a Christian consciousness, which is sadly missing in many of the churches that are growing.

TEACHING TO BUILD A VISIONARY CHRISTIAN CONSCIOUSNESS

In our time, there is a consumer consciousness in many churches, but a Christian consciousness is rare. Out of this Christian consciousness, agape love flows, the love that accepts people where they are and treats them there as if they were where they ought to be. The concerned minister will be alert to the need for resources, methods, and occasions for fostering this ordered approach to this perennial task, always eager to affect greater competency in this necessary work of the church.

I remember when I was given the charge of pastoring in Detroit. In the first business meeting that we held as a congregation, I asked them for permission to use the first three hours of every morning free from any encumbrances apart from an emergency that might arise, and I told them why. I told them I wanted to be in study, preparing for worship, exegeting passages so that I could gain the meaning of Scripture to share with them for their living, and I said, "I want to spend time in prayer so that when I come among you in my visitation at the hospital or in your home, my presence will count for something. It will be more than routine."

They agreed to give me the first three hours of the early morning free from any encumbrances, and that lasted for 25 years. I was fresh every Sunday and never had burnout. I am talking about a way of staying vital by means of being under the truth and scheduling times in such a way that our main business remains the main business. As a result of what happened in the midst of that kind of commitment we did not have room for the people who came to Bible study in the midweek hour. They were standing around the walls—teaching, teaching—sharing truth. A church develops integrity by being in touch with truth, where everyone sees himself or herself in that mirror, and so we know how we look. And we can appeal to God for change. Integrity.

VISIONARY IMPACT OF A HOLY EXAMPLE

By attitude and behavior, a pastor incarnates what the church is to be and how growth will take place. A pastor develops integrity most contagiously through his or her own personal Christian character and earnest example. The accent I am placing upon a personal life that can appeal to others is very important because unless we instruct out of a sense of integrity that is granted by the graciousness of the Lord, unless we do our work out of a disciplined direction by being under our Master in heaven, then whatever we do will not matter anyway. The character and the ability of the person in the pulpit will determine the nature of its work and the extent of its helpfulness.

Harold Carter—a pastor-friend in Baltimore, Maryland, well-known scholarly preacher whose education for ministry was gained at several of the leading theological seminaries in our country—commented in print some years ago: "I never heard the instructor in Christian ethics lecture on the basic morality that ought to be part and parcel of the Christian ministry." During any class in ministerial ethics, this should be consciously and intentionally done so that we understand the meaning of being a minister of the Word.

Aware that this need for moral character is so important and necessary that it should not be overlooked or left unmentioned, Carter devoted a whole chapter to this subject in his book *Myths That Mire the Ministry*. He warned against concupiscence, which he defined as that desire for temporal ends that has its seat in the senses. He further said, "Sex presents such a formidable problem in ministerial ranks, and since this is so, an in-depth study of its impact on our calling would be a blessing in seminary circles." Many seminaries now include the study of human sexuality among their required courses so we can understand our humanity and how to discipline it for the sake of integrity as we lead.

Now, some of those studies that are presently being offered include an inquiry into the problem of sexual promiscuity as not only a failure in morals—which it is—but sometimes a behavior disorder or an addiction. Male and female seminarians taking these courses are guided in studying themselves existentially, with a focus on understanding temptation, entanglements, the influence of moods, the problem of viewing other persons as objects, and the problem of a low-self-esteem that manifests itself in seeking to control other people. And none of these things, on the part of the minister, can help him or her minister with integrity. We must come back to that biblical notion of holiness, which in the Greek really means wholeness. We must be of one piece.

Given the scope and the import of ministering, a serious look at our own selfhood and the potential problem areas about which we must be aware is increasingly necessary. The ultimate response that vital ministry demands of you and of me is that of a God-committed selfhood, coupled with spiritual empowerment—more than methods, more than techniques, the self dominated and directed by the Holy Spirit.

In isolating some of the elements that grant this enablement and comprise a responsible moral life for us, John Malcus Ellison accented these: sincerity, honesty, unselfishness, loyalty to principle, loyalty to truth, and integrity. He added, "These have no substitutes in the religious leader. The Lord requires clean hands and honest hearts for His work. He always did, He still does, He always will."

A church that has integrity usually grows out of the ministry of a minister who has integrity. It has become rather commonplace to hear some minister commonly referred to as a great leader, meaning that he or she mixes well with people and handles leadership responsibilities with adequacy, with timeliness, and with a strong sense of selfhood. Many ministers view this great-leader image as worthy of their concern and their effort. I hope this is not the dream you are dreaming—being a great leader. I hope you are not content to be viewed as a great leader. I hope your dream includes developing leaders by your leadership and trying to make your other leaders great. And this requires the work of teaching.

Jesus showed the way in this as in all other necessary areas. Concerned about the future of the work to which He set himself, He envisioned, selected, and trained a small group to expand and perpetuate His service as teacher, preacher, and healer. The demands upon Him had become unending and excessive, and aware that He had impacted a growing number of followers, He finally identified and isolated from within the larger crowd those who showed the most avid openness to Him and seemed reasonably gifted for what He would require of them.

According to Luke 6:12-13, when the time came for Jesus to single out those persons from the crowd and shape them for assignments under His direction, He withdrew to pray about the choices He must make. He prayed about it all throughout the night, exploring His options with God, with a God-illumined thought process. And the account tells us that when day came, "He called His disciples and chose twelve from among them, whom He named apostles" (Luke 6:13, NRSV).

The rest of the Gospels tell us the subsequent training of the Twelve. They underscore the time and the guidance Jesus gave in shaping them for leadership. He was sensible about the work God had assigned to His hands. He chose and developed others to assist Him in handling tasks that are required in each generation. The pastor must operate according to this vision already cast by our Lord.

SHARE YOUR DREAM OF VISIONARY LEADERS WHO POSSESS INTEGRITY

Let us highlight the ministry and not our own individual ministry—*the* ministry, meaning all of us working together as partners, in team fashion, and not working as competitive figures with our own private dream. We serve the whole church a little at a time. Dream your dreams. Let them be big, but let them be the same dreams that our Lord had when He started the Church, to let it have integrity and to give His life for it.

It was a wise word that Roger Hazelton, former dean at Oberlin Graduate School of Theology, shared with his students. "The truly effective minister is not someone who can take oversight in the church but who can share insight with that church," he said. It is not one or the other; it is both. If we have insight, a church is more apt to give us and let us retain oversight. "Mark this," Hazelton said, "people in our churches today need more than strength for the mastery of life; they need light on the mystery of life, and there is a positive relationship between the two. In the last analysis, you cannot have the one without the other."

Develop great leaders. Pour your hearts into them. Do not allow yourself to be the central focus. Be the figure around whom the congregation coalesces, but let them coalesce for the right reason—receiving truth shared from the heart that is concerned about them, so concerned that you spare no pain in order to help them have integrity. Those who truly love the Lord and are deeply concerned to help people learn to live by God's will can develop churches with integrity because they will be contented, like that parson in Geoffrey Chaucer's *Canterbury Tales*, to gladly teach by following that teaching themselves.

This chapter is reprinted from *Leading with Vision* in the Beeson Pastoral Series, Dale Galloway, comp. (Kansas City: Beacon Hill Press of Kansas City, 1999), 27-41. Reprinted by permission.

Stan Toler is senior pastor of Trinity Church of the Nazarene in Oklahoma City and hosts the television program *Leadership Today*. For several years he has taught seminars for Dr. John Maxwell's INJOY Group—a leadership development institute. Toler has written over 50 books, including his best-sellers *God Has Never Failed Me, but He's Sure Scared Me to Death a Few Times*; *The Buzzards Are Circling, but God's Not Finished with Me Yet*; *The Five-Star Church*; his popular Minute Motivators series; and his latest book, *The Secret Blend*.

Jerry Brecheisen (pronounced "breck-eye-zen") is currently the managing editor of his denomination's magazine and producer of its international radio ministry, he traveled over 15 years in his family's gospel music ministry and served 28 years in pastoral ministry—22 years as senior pastor in multiple staff churches.

He has authored 11 books personally and has coauthored, edited, or compiled over 20 books for major publishers and well-known Christian personalities. He is a magazine columnist, has written numerous articles for Christian magazines, and regularly contributes to on-line magazines.

Jerry and his wife, Carol, reside in Indianapolis. They have two married children. They are also the proud grandparents of three.

3
Making Christ Your Pattern
Stan Toler and Jerry Brecheisen

A HISTORY PROFESSOR COMMENTED ON CHRISTOPHER COLUMBUS'S discovery of America, saying that there were three significant aspects of the trip. One, before he left, he didn't have a clue as to where he was going. Two, when he arrived, he didn't have a clue as to where he was. And three, when he got ready to leave, he didn't have a clue as to how to get back home.

From the back of the room a history major spoke up: "And four, he didn't have a clue as to how he was ever going to pay back that loan to the government!"

Thankfully, when it comes to Christian leadership, we can be a little more informed. We have the greatest leadership model.

The Lord Jesus Christ is God's final word on leadership.

He is the divine *Logos*. God the Father communicated leadership principles through His Son. Earth's greatest Leader was born on the wrong side of the tracks. He had no earthly office space—in fact, the birds of the air had better accommodations—and He never had an expense account. He didn't have an MBA from an Ivy League college, and *Fortune* magazine never featured Him. Nevertheless, He put His Creator skill on a self-sacrificing shelf and humbly learned to be an earthly leader at the side of a Nazareth carpenter's bench.

At His Jordan River baptism, God announced His approval of Him, and the Holy Spirit descended in power upon His human frame.

From there, Jesus of Nazareth led a few rough souls from the attics of obscurity to the pinnacles of Christian history. His God-blessed leadership mixed compassion with iron-willed tenacity. His words angered some and caused others to weep.

He encouraged. He chastised. He forgave. He spoke with authority and lived with authenticity. He never gave up on those whom He led—even if it meant His own death. Every leader would be wise to *learn* from Him, *live* like Him, and *follow* His leadership principles.

Whether you're leading by accident or appointment, there's hope in following the Master. Along with His disciples, He pounded some direction signs into the soil of their times that will help us in our journey.

THE GREAT PREREQUISITE FOR CHRISTIAN LEADERSHIP

The New Testament is a survival manual for people in the trenches of leadership.

Step one: Sincere personal faith. One of the most influential leaders in the New Testament was John the Baptist. Crowds of people pushed and shoved to hear the words of this straight-talking messenger of the Messiah who wore designer suits made of camel hair.

But what was the root of that influence? According to John 1:23, when the religious leaders asked for his credentials, "John replied in the words of Isaiah the prophet, 'I am the voice of one calling in the desert, "Make straight the way for the Lord."'"

John the Baptist knew who he was. He had heavenly connections. His leadership strengths didn't come from books or seminars, conferences or conventions. As vital as those edge-sharpening times may be, John's greatest leadership strengths came from the power and promises focused on and flowing from the Messiah. And his message to the masses about the Christ was always the same: "He must become greater; I must become less" (John 3:30).

Our real power for leadership is in our connection to heaven—in surrendering to and gaining strength from the power of a risen Christ. That's seen in these powerful words of His:

> I am the true vine, and my Father is the gardener. He cuts off every branch in me that bears no fruit, while every branch that does bear fruit he prunes so that it will be even more fruitful. You are already clean because of the word I have spoken to you. Remain in me, and I will remain in you. No branch can bear fruit by itself; it must remain in the vine. Neither can you bear fruit unless you remain in me. I am the vine; you are the branches. If a man remains in me and I in him, he will bear much fruit; apart from me you can do nothing (*John 15:1-5*).

The scores of laypersons that have been trained in the evangelism and discipleship methods of Campus Crusade for Christ International have heard that scriptural mandate over and over: "Apart from me you can do nothing."

Faith in Christ is the channel of spiritual life for leaders!

A Christian leader will never lead people forward for Christ without first taking his or her own trip to the Cross. Without the electricity of Calvary's flow, human leaders are powerless.

Twentieth-century songwriter Jessie B. Pounds said it well:

I must needs go home by the way of the cross;
There's no other way but this.
I shall ne'er get sight of the Gates of Light
If the way of the cross I miss.

There is no bypass. Anyone who would seek to influence others for Christ must take a direct route to the Cross. A personal faith in the Lord Jesus Christ (John 1:12) is the great prerequisite for Christian leadership.

MAKE SURE THE CAPTAIN IS AT THE CONTROLS

During a commuter flight the plane seemed to bounce excessively. Wanting to soothe the nerves of the concerned passengers, the pilot walked from the cockpit and stood in the aisle to make an announcement: "Ladies and gentlemen, there's nothing to worry about. We're just having a little problem with engine number two. In fact, I'll be honest with you—the engine has quit running. But you'll be glad to know that we have three other engines that are working properly."

Walking toward the cockpit, the pilot suddenly turned around and said, "Oh, I almost forgot. You'll also be relieved to know that we have three pastors on board this flight."

Loud enough for everyone in the tiny commuter plane to hear, the passenger in the front row turned to his seatmate and said, "I don't know about you, but I'd just as soon have four good engines!"

Even with four good engines, some flights are bouncy and unpredictable. Sometimes there are weather delays that affect the arrival. Sometimes there are miscalculations about fuel supply. Sometimes there's simply too much baggage on board.

But whatever the problem may be, you can be assured that the final responsibility is the captain's. Without his or her control, the whole flight is somewhat endangered.

It may be elementary, but it's a vital lesson on leadership. All the engines of organizational programs, property, or personnel are ultimately endangered unless the Captain, Christ, is at the controls. "Apart from me you can do nothing" (John 15:5).

So Christian leadership begins with an evaluation of its dependence on the Captain. "Search me, O God, and know my heart" (Ps. 139:23). Until the *heart* of the leader is right before God, the *works* of the leader will ultimately be ineffective.

God calls the leader to a quiet place—away from the noise of non-essentials—and invites him or her to look over the spiritual checklist. Here are some items that might be on it:

- "Is Christ the Lord of my life?"
- "Am I trying to operate on His strength or my own?"
- "Do I consistently seek the wisdom of His Word?"
- "Do I talk to Him in prayer before I talk to the people?"
- "Am I relying on the power of His Holy Spirit?"
- "Are there hidden things in my life that I need to confess to Him?"
- "Am I in fellowship with His people?"
- "Is He first in my planning process?"
- "Do my programs and methods honor Him?"

Hudson T. Armerding, former president of Wheaton College, wrote, "The Christian leader must determine that he will go God's way and not make his decisions on the basis of such considerations as his relationship with the hierarchy, or his financial reward, or his status. Furthermore, he must be spiritually discerning in his willingness to identify himself with the people of God."[1]

God's way.

God's people.

Sounds a lot like Christian leadership—the kind of leadership intent on moving people forward when they're standing still!

FOLLOW THE LEADER'S LEADERSHIP

God's Word on leadership is seen in the practices and priorities of Jesus Christ. The disciplines and patterns of His life affected His leadership. His character traits modeled the best of Christian leadership. And His absolute sincerity set the course for His earthly ministry.

1. Jesus Was Sincere in His Purpose

Jesus of Nazareth had divine direction. He was always aware of a higher purpose, always moving toward Calvary. The Master was on a monumental mission to buy back the souls claimed by Satan in Eden's yard sale.

"The Son of Man came to seek and to save what was lost" (Luke 19:10).

So everything He did in that tiny window of time on earth (three short years) moved Him toward fulfilling His calling.

Even as a child, He had a sense of duty that loomed above the daily regimens of His life. During the Feast of the Passover celebration in Jerusalem, a 12-year-old Jesus became separated from His parents.

Upon finding Him in the Temple among religious leaders and teachers, Jesus' parents corrected Him for wandering away. But He had wandered only from their watchful eye—not from the way, not from the path that His Heavenly Father had carved out of the forests of time. He replied to Mary and Joseph, "Why were you searching for me? . . . Didn't you know I had to be in my Father's house?" (2:49). He was where He belonged, doing what He was born to do—ministering to people.

There was an absolute purity in Jesus' purpose. Above all, He sincerely sought His Father's will for the redemption of humanity. "Not my will, but yours be done" (22:42).

In the classic Sherlock Holmes whodunit novel *Scandal in Bohemia,* Watson is pressed into service to witness the marriage of the protagonist. In a typically twisted turn of events, the newly married couple drives off from the cathedral site of their marriage of convenience in different carriages. Watson's observations of the events surprisingly describe many organizations—Christian or otherwise—"They drove away in different directions, and I went off to make my own arrangements."

Christian leadership without direction or purpose is dangerous at best. Many "gospel ships" have wrecked on the rocks of time because some sailor neglected to set the sails properly.

Christlike leadership always focuses on the main thing.

What is it? *Redemption.*

Jesus spelled it out for us in His prayer to the Father for His disciples, "As you sent me into the world, I have sent them into the world" (John 17:18).

Every Christian leader already has a direction, a purpose: to bring people to the Kingdom, to a personal and vital faith in the Lord Jesus Christ. That's the bottom line—now and forever.

Everything else is incidental. Packing people into pews or adding stepstools on organizational flow charts isn't what it's all about.

There's no better job description than that found in the Great Commission (Matt. 28:18-20).

Direction is of utmost importance. There is a dynamic in a destination.

When we leave our home and go out the front door, we don't usually announce to our friends or loved ones, "I'm going anywhere—be back sometime!"

Our direction is usually a bit more specific. We start out for "somewhere," not "anywhere." "Somewhere" has a cohesive direction to it—a certain place, an estimated arrival, a prescribed route. "Anywhere" is confusing, aimless, and haphazard.

It's said that professional ice hockey great Wayne Gretzky "was better at the game of hockey, perhaps, than anyone ever because he knew where the puck was going, not just where it had been. Turn out the lights in the middle of a play, his coach said, and Gretzky would still know where every player was on the ice."[2]

People who are "standing still" obviously lack direction. They are "anywhere" folks rather than "somewhere" folks. They are happy with the haphazard and content with the confusing. In a "revised version" of the well-known gospel song, they seem to be "leaning on the everlasting *charms.*" They are deceptively charmed by their inertia, mesmerized by their motionlessness. They like *who* they are, *what* they are, and *where* they are well enough not to bother moving.

If you would be a leader who moves people forward, you'll need a sincere purpose. You'll need to understand exactly *why* you're doing *what* you're intending to do. And then you'll bravely move in that direction.

The sheer synergy of direction is bound to set a few tennis shoes or wing tips in motion!

Redemption was of ultimate importance to the Lord Jesus Christ.

Every event in the busyness of Jesus' day was a redemptive act. Every earthly activity had the ultimate end of sacrifice and surrender to fulfill the higher purpose of bringing people to the Kingdom. "As the time approached for him to be taken up to heaven, Jesus resolutely set out for Jerusalem" (Luke 9:51).

There was a hidden agenda in His every act of leadership; there was a "Cross reference" in everything.

What's your purpose?

- To further the kingdom of God *or* to gain personal recognition?
- To establish Christians in their faith *or* to gather loyalty to yourself?
- To build up the church of Christ *or* to build a personal kingdom?

Which of your objectives need to be discarded? Which need to be developed?

Christlike leadership is more than leading people from Point A to Point B. It's more than working through some corporate to-do list. It's a commitment of the heart to offer oneself to help others become everything that God intended.

The wedding ceremony had reached the moment of lighting the unity candle. The bride and groom moved from the altar up to the candle on the platform.

The pastor whispered instructions to the couple just to make sure they remembered what to do: "Each of you take the candles on the outside, light the center candle together, and then blow out your individual candles."

The pastor then explained to the audience that the blowing out of the two outer candles represented the couple's surrender of their individual freedom.

The groom suddenly thought about the significance of the act and whispered back to the pastor, "Would it be all right if we just blow out her candle?"

Obviously the apostle Paul had blown his candle out. He had a strong sense of purpose that found its fulfillment in surrendering to Christ:

> Whatever was to my profit I now consider loss for the sake of Christ. What is more, I consider everything a loss compared to the surpassing greatness of knowing Christ Jesus my Lord, for whose sake I have lost all things. I consider them rubbish, that I may gain Christ and be found in him, not having a righteousness of my own that comes from the law, but that which is through faith in Christ —the righteousness that comes from God and is by faith. I want to know Christ and the power of his resurrection and the fellowship of sharing in his sufferings, becoming like him in his death, and so, somehow, to attain to the resurrection from the dead.
>
> Not that I have already obtained all this, or have already been made perfect, but I press on to take hold of that for which Christ Jesus took hold of me. Brothers, I do not consider myself yet to have taken hold of it. But one thing I do: Forgetting what is behind and straining toward what is ahead, I press on toward the goal to win the prize for which God has called me heavenward in Christ Jesus (*Phil. 3:7-14*).

2. Jesus Was Sincere in His Service to Others

It was just before the Passover Feast. Jesus knew that the time had come for him to leave this world and go to the Father. Having loved his own who were in the world, he now showed them the full extent of his love.

The evening meal was being served, and the devil had already prompted Judas Iscariot, son of Simon, to betray Jesus. Jesus knew that the Father had put all things under his power, and that he had come from God and was returning to God; so he got up from the meal, took off his outer clothing, and wrapped a towel around his waist. After that, he poured water into a basin and began to wash his disciples' feet, drying them with the towel that was wrapped around him.

He came to Simon Peter, who said to him, "Lord, are you going to wash my feet?"

Jesus replied, "You do not realize now what I am doing, but later you will understand."

"No," said Peter, "you shall never wash my feet."

Jesus answered, "Unless I wash you, you have no part with me."

"Then, Lord," Simon Peter replied, "not just my feet but my hands and my head as well!"

Jesus answered, "A person who has had a bath needs only to wash his feet; his whole body is clean. And you are clean, though not every one of you." For he knew who was going to betray him, and that was why he said not every one was clean.

When he had finished washing their feet, he put on his clothes and returned to his place. "Do you understand what I have done for you?" he asked them. "You call me 'Teacher' and 'Lord,' and rightly so, for that is what I am. Now that I, your Lord and Teacher, have washed your feet, you also should wash one another's feet. I have set you an example that you should do as I have done for you" (John 13:1-15).

If you're looking for a leadership model, you've found it. Jesus of Nazareth should have been on the receiving end of that foot washing! Everything that exists came from His hand. He owns the stars. He planted every blade of grass. He applied the golden hue to every field flower. He pointed the rays of the sun to a million darkened valleys. He deserved to be treated like royalty. Instead, He grabbed a towel and taught some astonished disciples how to motivate others by loving and serving them.

Understand the significance of service. God-inspired, Spirit-empowered, loving service is one of the great motivators.

A family with fussy kids had been traveling all day in a sport utility vehicle.

The father's dour face told its own story as he dutifully went into a seafood restaurant and asked the waitress, "Lady, do you serve crabs here?"

She took one look at the grumpy traveler and quickly responded, "Sure! We'll serve anyone. Have a seat, and I'll be right with you!"

Vibrant leadership looks to the grateful or the grumpy and says, "Have a seat, and I'll be right with you."

Granted, many times the Christian leader feels more like wielding a stick rather than a towel! The stubbornness, childishness, carnality, and lethargy of others are characteristics that haunt the leader and hinder progress.

Jesus was not immune to such behavior. The New Testament pathways were crowded with careless, crude, or crummy pedestrians. Even His disciples had their pouting spells, attention-grabbings, *get-ahead-aches*, and spiritual mob rule.

Someone once said, "Every group has at least one difficult person in it. If you don't immediately recognize who that person is, it's probably you!"

Just like any leader, Jesus faced the disappointments of working with people who failed to live up to their potential, who didn't keep their promises, who put themselves first over the greater cause.

Even His closest associates misunderstood His calling. For example, when Jesus talked about a "kingdom," His disciples were thinking about an earthly "democracy" instead of a heavenly "theocracy."

You'll remember that at the glorious moment of His transfiguration, His inner circle of disciples tried to turn its beauty into a building program!

> After six days Jesus took Peter, James and John with him and led them up a high mountain, where they were all alone. There he was transfigured before them. His clothes became dazzling white, whiter than anyone in the world could bleach them. And there appeared before them Elijah and Moses, who were talking with Jesus. Peter said to Jesus, "Rabbi, it is good for us to be here. Let us put up three shelters—one for you, one for Moses and one for Elijah" (*Mark 9:2-5*).

It was the same bunch that tried to stop Jesus from washing their feet and thereby expressing His love and duty to them. Instead of handing out layoff notices, Jesus chose to extend a towel. Instead of berating, He chose a blessing. And the hearts of His followers melted like a snow cone under an Oklahoma summer sun.

Jesus always looked beyond the imperfections of His colleagues to their potential. He taught us the advantages of acceptance, the incentive of kindness, and the lasting influence of sincere love and service.

- He always accepted people as they were and helped them become better.
- He understood that God-given abilities are stored in jars of clay.
- He focused on restoration and healing, bringing honor out of the flaws.

One of the great love stories in history is that of Winston Churchill and his beloved wife, Clemmie. Biographer James C. Humes gives a vivid example: "At a very formal gathering, Churchill was asked, 'If you could not be who you are, who would you like to be?' Churchill responded, 'If I could not be who I am, I would most like to be'—and here he paused to take his wife's hand—'Lady Churchill's second husband.'"[3]

As an honored guest in the midst of an elaborate ceremony, the great leader chose to focus on the person whom he loved. Most everything else that happened on that occasion has been forgotten, but the devotion of a husband to his wife has lived on.

You'll never rise so high as when you stoop to give honor and service to another. Madeleine L'Engle was quoted in PreachingToday.com: "Following Christ has nothing to do with success as the world sees success. It has to do with love."[4]

John the Baptist said, "He must become greater; I must become less" (John 3:30). And the influence that matters is His love and presence working its wonderful way through the actions and attitudes of the Christian leader.

3. Jesus Was Sincere in His Communications

Leith Anderson said, "Leadership is about leaders, followers, organizations, circumstances, power, history, and more. It is the relationship of each to the other that makes the leadership matrix."[5]

And there is no relationship without communication. The best-laid plans are worthless unless they're communicated to others. The best-intentioned feelings are useless to another unless they're expressed. Leaders must be able to express themselves.

But those expressions must be carefully thought out, and they must have a redemptive purpose. Many communicators have learned the hard way that some comments are better left unsaid—especially within range of the microphone. One radio announcer on a Christian radio station commented to his engineer without knowing that the microphone was still live, "I shouldn't have put that Tabasco sauce on my eggs this morning." Then, in probably his most embarrassing broadcast moment, he emitted the belch heard 'round the world!

Jesus didn't make statements that shouldn't be heard when the microphone was on. His communication was sound, purposeful, and redemptive.

Whenever Jesus spoke in public, His speech had a redeeming value. Even when He spoke harshly to the spiritual hypocrites of His day, it came from an impassioned heart of acceptance and love. Naturally—His speech was a reflection of His character.

With His speech, He lifted people from their dungeons of despair. For example, to a guilty adulteress He gave the declaration of her independence.

> The teachers of the law and the Pharisees brought in a woman caught in adultery. They made her stand before the group and said to Jesus, "Teacher, this woman was caught in the act of adultery. In the Law Moses commanded us to stone such women. Now what do you say?" They were using this question as a trap, in order to have a basis for accusing him.
>
> But Jesus bent down and started to write on the ground with his finger. When they kept on questioning him, he straightened up and said to them, "If any one of you is without sin, let him be the first to throw a stone at her." Again he stooped down and wrote on the ground.
>
> At this, those who heard began to go away one at a time, the older ones first, until only Jesus was left, with the woman still standing there. Jesus straightened up and asked her, "Woman, where are they? Has no one condemned you?"
>
> "No one, sir," she said.
>
> "Then neither do I condemn you," Jesus declared. "Go now and leave your life of sin" *(John 8:3-11)*.

With His speech Jesus gave hope to the helpless. One day as He taught, a group of friends lowered a crippled young man from the roof into the very room where Jesus stood. He was brought there expecting to receive a miracle. Instead, he got two. In mercy, Jesus mingled healing with forgiveness in the life of the helpless. And with a word, the young man's life was forever changed. When the religious leaders questioned His actions, Jesus was patient enough to answer: "'That you may know that the Son of Man has authority on earth to forgive sins. . . .' He said to the paralyzed man, 'I tell you, get up, take your mat and go home'" (Luke 5:24).

With His speech He motivated people to use their talents for the Kingdom. "No one lights a lamp and hides it in a jar or puts it under a bed. Instead, he puts it on a stand, so that those who come in can see the light" (8:16).

But whenever He spoke, it was with sincerity and love.

Paul Davidson wrote in USA Today about a group of computer hackers who made a break with their dishonest past to work for a computer security firm and eventually were hired as consultants by the government. Called "L0pht," the computer specialists boasted to a Senate committee of being able to shut down the Internet in 30 minutes. Davidson wrote, "L0pht members describe themselves as 'gray hats,' on the edge between good and evil hackers."[6]

There's no room for "gray hats" in Christian leadership. If you're to call people forward in this millennium, even when they're standing still, you'll commit yourself to sincerity in your communication as well as in your conduct.

The power of a promise. You'll discover the power of a promise— the influence of keeping your word. People are motivated by Christian leaders who always try to do what they say they will. Vibrant Christian leaders understand that once a promise is given, people are waiting for the action.

Granted, that's not always possible. Circumstances sometimes seal off the promised actions like orange cones on a construction project. Sometimes the leader simply can't deliver on a promise. The promise was made too hastily; events caused a detour; facts and figures have changed. But the sincerity remains.

The Wonderful Worth of Words

If you haven't already, you'll discover the fantastic power of words. Words can be used either as *bombs* or *bouquets*. Which would you rather receive at your doorstep? A few words and sentences can be forged together and lobbed into the life of another to cause as much havoc as a two-year-old at a tea party.

Conversely, you can put approximately the same amount of words and sentences together to hand a discouraged worker a "speech bouquet." In fact, "Thank you—I appreciate you" is better *said* than shown!

And words that don't lift simply ought to be left alone.

The Test of Sincere Communication

And speaking of microphones . . .

"Test, one, two. Test, one, two. Is this on?"

Most people think Christian singers and speakers can count only to two! Every meeting or concert usually begins with a sound check.

How about a sincerity check? How will you know when your communication is "sincere"? New Testament leader Paul said, "Let your conversation be always full of grace, seasoned with salt, so that you may know how to answer everyone" (Col. 4:6).

Here are some questions to use as guidelines:

- Is it honest without being petty?
- Will it bring hope or help, or will it bring hurt?
- Will the giver and the receiver be better because of it?
- Does it reflect the attitude of Jesus Christ?
- Will the receiver learn something positive from the communication?

Shady communication and see-through promises never pay dividends—only division.

The story is told of two college students who were to take a final exam. Instead of studying, they took the time to go to town for a party.

The next morning, they overslept and missed the exam. Going to their professor, they made up a very convincing and heartbreaking story of how they had gone to visit an aunt of one of the students who was ill in a nearby hospital.

"It was awful, Prof," the students explained. "After we left that poor invalid woman, we rushed home to study for our exam. It was pouring down rain, and suddenly we had a flat tire along a very busy expressway."

"Stop!" the professor interrupted. "You can make up the exam tomorrow."

The next day, the students arrived at the professor's classroom. He quickly put them in two different rooms and handed them an exam. The first part of the exam was a breeze. The note at the top of the exam paper said that Part 1 was worth 30 points.

There was also a note at the bottom: "Turn this page over for the rest of the exam—*worth 70 points*."

Part 2 was on the other side. It was a "fill-in-the-blank" question that caused instant anxiety for the students in their separate rooms: "Which tire went flat on your trip to see that invalid aunt?"[7]

4. Jesus Was Sincere in His Relationships

The Gospel writers counted 5,000 men. With women and children added, the number was probably at least three times that amount. Sitting on the sunny slope of a Judean mountain, they had no idea that the sermon they were hearing would be called the greatest of history—the Sermon on the Mount. Jesus included points about meekness that turns to an inheritance, poverty that owns a kingdom, and humility that blossoms into exaltation. Timeless truths poked their heads through windows of narration, object lessons, humor, and drama.

What a magnificent day!

What a magnificent storyteller, this Nazarene!

Was it His greatest sermon? Probably. But it wasn't His only sermon. There were so many others that touched the hearts and minds of those who followed Him.

One was only heard by an audience that was tiny compared to the thousands who had heard Him on that other mountain.

This mountain scene was far removed from sunny slopes and gentle waves that caressed the trembling shores of Galilee. This sermon could barely be heard above the angry shouts of a bloodthirsty mob on Golgotha.

> Near the cross of Jesus stood his mother, his mother's sister, Mary the wife of Clopas, and Mary Magdalene. When Jesus saw his mother there, and the disciple whom he loved standing nearby, he said to his mother, "Dear woman, here is your son," and to the disciple, "Here is your mother." From that time on, this disciple took her into his home (*John 19:25-27*).

This wasn't a sermon about lights hid under bushels or hearts pure enough to see God. This was about duty. A son would soon die and leave a mother without any means of support.

Devotion won out over the commotion.

Love ruled in the face of unspeakable anger.

With one act of mercy, the greatest leader who ever lived taught His followers how to sincerely put relationship above responsibilities: "Dear woman, here is your son." And to His dear friend He gave the task of caring for the woman who bore the Messiah.

It could truly be said of Jesus that He was a "people person." He sat down to dinner with Lazarus, Martha, and Mary at Bethany. Friends and loved ones were dear to His heart.

Relationships above responsibilities. He was concerned with His earthly duties. He practiced the carpenter trade. He hung out with fishermen. He gave some of His greatest insights from the examples seen in the sheepherding and agriculture communities. But He involved himself with those vocations to touch the lives of their people. He was concerned that fishers of *fish* become fishers of *men*.

Jay C. Grelen wrote an on-line article about basketball superstar David Robinson. After the statistics were quoted, the trophies had been counted, and the accomplishments had been acknowledged, Grelen focused on what really mattered in the life of the 7-foot-1 San Antonio Spurs standout: His family and friends. "He is more concerned that his three boys learn godly character than whether they can match his Top 10 ranking in the NBA for points, rebounds, and blocked shots per game. He is more concerned that his fans see him live out his faith than he is interested in talking about the time in 1994 that he scored 71 points against the Los Angeles Clippers."[8]

Faith. Family. Friends. Those are the lasting things.

"Let's get a move on!" an anxious husband reminded his wife as the family scurried about for the journey to Sunday School.

The tension in the room soon began to thicken like day-old bubble gum. "What?" the mother asked sharply.

The husband spoke softer and more deliberately: "I just wondered if we could try not to be late again this Sunday."

"OK," the wife replied sharply. "Let's do a trade-off next week."

"A trade-off?"

"Yep!" the wife continued. "Next week you cook breakfast, dress the kids, let the dog out, gather all the Sunday School quarterlies, get dinner ready . . . and I'll sit in the car, honk the horn, and shake my watch in the window!"[9]

Obviously harmony in the home should have been a priority over punctuality at the church. Now, that's not an indictment against punctuality, especially when tardiness seems to be gaining ground over baseball as the national pastime.

But Christian leaders cannot forget the Golgotha scene. Relationships are more important than responsibilities. Right in the midst of the most trying time of His life, Jesus focused on His family duties.

Whether a Christian leader builds a church or organization is ultimately not as important as whether he or she focuses on building a home. Paul asked a haunting question that rings in the ears of new millennium leaders: "If anyone does not know how to manage his own family, how can he take care of God's church?" (1 Tim. 3:5).

Never neglect your own family in your service to others.

Family life must not be an afterthought. Fifty years from this point in your life, times with your immediate family will generate greater memories than a packed auditorium on Friend Day.

A famous actor known for his devotion to his family, once said, "I make a lot of money and I've given a lot of it to charities, but I've given all of myself to my wife and the kids, and that's the best donation I'll ever make."

A sincere devotion to duty—including family duties—doesn't escape the glances of people for whom you're responsible. That devotion could be the very incentive that sparks them to start a "renovation project" in their own homes. And the resulting improvements there could very well extend to your church or organization.

Notes

1. Hudson T. Armerding, *Leadership* (Wheaton, Ill.: Tyndale House Publishers, 1978), 26.

2. Bruce B. Auster, "A Legend on Ice," *U.S. News and World Report*, 6 December 1999, 22.

3. James C. Humes, *Churchill: Speaker of the Century* (New York: Stein and Day, 1980), 291.

4. Madeleine L'Engle, *Walking on Water: Reflections on Faith and Art,* quoted in "How Jesus Defines Success," PreachingToday.com, 20 February 2000, 1.

5. Leith Anderson, *Leadership That Works* (Minneapolis: Bethany House, 1999), 44.

6. Paul Davidson, "Hackers Join the Other Side," *USA Today*, 6 January 2000, A 1.

7. Source unknown.

8. Jay C. Grelen (Oct. 25, 1998), "Why Everyone Looks Up to David Robinson" <http://www.christianity.net/cr/8R2/8R2020.html>.

9. Anderson, *Leadership That Works*, 68.

This chapter is reprinted from Stan Toler and Jerry Brecheisen, *Lead to Succeed: New Testament Principles for Visionary Leadership* (Kansas City: Beacon Hill Press of Kansas City, 2003), 11-27, 123. Reprinted by permission.

Robert Leslie Holmes is pastor of First Presbyterian Church, Pittsburgh. He is a contributing editor to *Preaching: The Professional Journal for Those Who Preach* and the author of a number of books. The latest, *The Creed: Life Principles for Today* (Ambassador-Emerald Int'l) examines the Apostles' Creed in the light of postmodernism. You may reach him at rlholmes@fpcp.org.

4
Kingdom Excellence
When Good Enough Simply Isn't!
Robert Leslie Holmes

*"If anything is excellent or praiseworthy—
think about such things" (Phil. 4:8).*

🕊 **"IT'S CLOSE ENOUGH FOR GOVERNMENT WORK,"** he said to his helper. That may be true for the government, but this is no ordinary government housing. This is the house of the King of Kings. I decided then and there this workman's handiwork deserved a little closer inspection than I had perhaps planned to give it. Sure enough, "close enough for government work" defined a poor quality of workmanship on our project from start to finish: corners were not square, gaps showed at door bottoms, and windows were not sealed. For the man who did that work, getting by was acceptable. He did not realize that good enough simply is not good enough for God. What is more, he seemed not to realize that his example would do nothing to inspire his young assistant to try harder. Hence, the workman failed not only in achieving excellence but also as a mentor. His unwillingness to reach for excellence may well produce inferior workmanship in generations still to come.

THE CULT OF SECOND BEST

This chapter calls us to recognize that good enough simply isn't and that this is never truer than when we are about God's business. "Praise the LORD! Praise God in His sanctuary; praise Him in His mighty expanse. Praise Him for His mighty deeds; praise Him according to His excellent greatness" (Ps. 150:1-2, NASB). The message seems plain enough: If God has blessed us with excellence all through His creation, surely we should use that as a model for our own praise.

Tragically, the same spirit of "good enough" that the construction worker tried to pass off that day prevails in the church. We have turned

51

the church of the Most High God into a cult where second best is acceptable. We celebrate mediocrity and wonder why many people consider us insignificant or why the church has lost its moral influence over society. "The society which scorns excellence in plumbing because plumbing is a humble activity and tolerates shoddiness in philosophy because it is an exalted activity will have neither good plumbing nor good philosophy. Neither its pipes nor its theories will hold water," declared John Gardner.[1] The fact remains that our society demands excellence in our appearance and our products—hence the billions of dollars that are invested annually into research and development by corporations of all sizes—yet in the church we often seem content to give second best.

EXCELLENCE!

"An excellent wife is the crown of her husband" (Prov. 12:4, NASB). If this principle is true for the secular world, how much more so should Christ's Bride—the Church that bears His name—pursue excellence! Just what is excellence? And how can we cultivate a spirit of excellence in the church of Jesus Christ in the 21st century? In this chapter, I propose to look at excellence under three general headings: first, a brief discussion of the meanings and uses of the words "excellent" and "excellence" in Scripture; second, a word about how pastors might apply what the Bible says in their individual ministries; and third, an observation about how laypeople might appropriate what Scripture says in their local church settings.

EXCELLENCE DEFINED

Both Old Testament Hebrew and New Testament Greek help us to discern what God has in mind when His Word speaks about excellence or the quality of being excellent. The Hebrew *gaon* is chiefly related to the idea of swelling or growing greater. In a variety of forms, this word calls us to rise above the norm and is translated in a context that speaks of being above, of superabundance and surpassing elevation. One example is, "To Him who rides upon the highest heavens, which are from ancient times; behold, He speaks forth with His voice, a mighty voice. Ascribe strength to God; His majesty is over Israel; and His strength is in the skies" (Ps. 68:33-34, NASB). The idea is that God rises above the heavens, or literally "in heaven's heavens," that is, above all things. In the New Testament, the same idea is conveyed by the use of the Greek *perisseuo* and *huperecho*. In every instance, it speaks of going past the norm. Thus we can define excellence as going beyond the ordinary, or as Booker T. Washington reportedly defined it for his students, "Excellence is to do a common thing in an uncommon way."[2] Our English words—"excel," "excellent," "excellence"—do not find their root in ancient Hebrew or Greek but in the Latin word _excello_, meaning "to rise above, surpass."

One of Latin ancestry who understood the concept of _excello_ was Antonio Stradivari of Milan. For nearly four centuries, the Latinized version of his name, Stradivarius, has been synonymous with superior violins. Rare are those connoisseurs of fine musical instruments who do not agree that "a Stradivarius" is the nearest thing to perfection that has ever been achieved in any musical instrument of any kind. And for good reason—Stradivari firmly resolved that no instrument of his would leave his shop until it was as near to perfection as human hands could make it. For him, being "good enough" was never good enough. Today, nearly 400 years after he was born in Cremona, Milan, his instruments are the very definition of excellence; they are the standard by which other violins are measured. Once Stradivari is said to have observed, "God needs violins to send his music into the world and if any violins are defective then God's music will be spoiled." His philosophy of work was summed up in a simple phrase, "Other men will make other violins, but no man shall make a better one."[3] Antonio Stradivari knew the meaning of excellence—to do the ordinary in an extraordinary way, to rise above what others call acceptable.

Rising above the ordinary means rising before the ordinary and soaring above ordinariness every morning at Paul Harvey's house in West Suburban River Forest near Chicago. The alarm clock rings at 3:30 A.M., and Paul Harvey's daily routine kicks in like clockwork: brush teeth, shower, shave, get dressed, eat oatmeal, get into car, and drive downtown. It all takes a well-organized 45 minutes or so. Paul Harvey dresses formally to report for work—shirt, coat, and tie—not in the often slovenly manner common to many radio performers. "It is all about discipline," Harvey says. "I could go to work in my pajamas, but long ago I got some advice from the engineer for my friend Billy Graham's radio show. If you don't [use discipline] in every area, you'll lose your edge."[4] Paul Harvey sees himself as God's servant. He understands the idea of giving our best to the One who gave His Son for us. It is no wonder then that he chuckled as he delivered this:

> The Butterball turkey company sets up a telephone hotline during the holidays to answer consumer questions about preparing turkeys. Once a woman called and asked about cooking a turkey

that had been lying on her freezer bottom for 23 years! The Butterball representative told her the turkey would probably be safe to eat if the freezer had been kept below zero for the entire 23 years. But the Butterball representative admitted that even if the turkey were safe to eat, its flavor would likely have deteriorated so much that she would not recommend eating it. The caller replied, "That's what I thought. We'll give the turkey to our church!"

It was a case of giving something not good enough for her family to the family of God, a kind of modern Ananias and Sapphira story.[5]

"Whatever you do, work at it with all your heart, as working for the Lord, not for men, since you know that you will receive an inheritance from the Lord as a reward. It is the Lord Christ you are serving" (Col. 3:23-24). The recognition that all our work is an act of worship should inspire us to soar above drudgery and reach for our best in everything. This means striving tomorrow to be better than we were today and then striving the day after that to be better again. It calls for matching our performance with our potential. Excellence is never an accident. It only happens when we determine to make it happen. People stumble into mediocrity, but no one ever stumbles into excellence, because excellence never happens by happenstance. The road to second best is easy to find. You can even find it without looking for a signpost, and it is never far away. Excellence, on the other hand, is harder to achieve; we get there by the sweat of our brow over a long period of time. As Ted W. Engstrom says in his fine book *The Pursuit of Excellence*, "All excellence involves discipline and tenacity of purpose."[6] Paul Harvey knows this. That's why—even in his 80s—he still sets that alarm clock for 3:30 every morning.

A word of caution is in order here. "Excellence" and "perfection" are not synonyms. To pursue perfection is different from pursuing excellence. Chasing after perfection can, and often does, result in neurosis and frustration. Going after excellence, on the other hand, is a healthy thing, a good exercise for mind and body. When perfection is achieved, the result will sometimes be a sense of despair because there are no more mountains to climb. Alexander the Great, for example, supposedly wept when he realized there were no more worlds to conquer. On the other hand, when excellence is achieved there is a sense of accomplishment and gratification.

Nor is excellence about being the best. It is about giving your best. If it were about being the best, there would be only one excellent person in every profession, one excellent church in God's kingdom, one excellent preacher in all the world. When you are the best at something, the reality is that there is only one way to go and it's down. When it is excellence you are after, the only way is up.

EXCELLENCE IN MINISTRY

"Praise the LORD in song, for He has done excellent things; let this be known throughout the earth" (Isa. 12:5, NASB). There is finally only one way for the church to tell the news of God's excellence throughout the earth, and that is for us to resolve to give Him nothing short of our best (as opposed to "the" best). We must come to realize that mediocrity has never yet inspired anyone to do anything worthwhile. The good news is that we can choose whether we will settle for halfhearted mediocrity or strive for excellence. Like that workman at our church, we can determine whether we become mediocre handymen or enthusiastic craftsmen in the pursuit of excellence. Indeed, it all begins at the point of choosing, and our choice will bear witness to our attitude. Someone has said that no one ever died from overwork but many have died from undermotivation. Surely the saddest people of all at the end of life are those who step out into eternity knowing they have offered up something less than their best and now it is too late to make amends.

The call to excellence—to do our best—as leaders is reflected in these words that come at one of the most important moments in Israel's history. "'May the LORD, the God of the spirits of all mankind, appoint a man over this community to go out and come in before them, one who will lead them out and bring them in, so the LORD's people will not be like sheep without a shepherd.' So the LORD said to Moses, 'Take Joshua son of Nun, a man in whom is the spirit, and lay your hand on him'" (Num. 27:16-18). A new day is dawning. Moses, knowing that his time is short, does not want to leave his sheep without a shepherd. He asks God to appoint a leader to lead both the internal and external affairs of the children of Israel. God's response to Moses' prayer is Joshua, "a man in whom is the spirit." I believe a fair paraphrase could say, "a man in whom is the desire to lead the people to a new level." In short, Joshua would not be satisfied with the status quo.

Excellence begins with a willing heart. The first call for a leader who would be excellent is to have this spirit of giving the best he or she is capable of giving. The spirit of excellence never enters any organization until it first possesses the leader. Down through the ages, this has been the case among those God has used to maximize their impact on His work and influence the future direction of His people. And it never has been more vital than in these first days of the third millennium. This is what the 21st century demands of its pastors and preachers, that is, a desire for excellence—excellence in faith and commitment. Not excuse! Not complaint! Not compromise! Not a willingness to get by with second best!

The *New York Times* reports that faith is fading fast among European Roman Catholics.[7] A primary reason cited is the failure of the Catholic Church in Europe to attract new priests. The shortage has reached crisis levels. It is not European Catholics alone who struggle with this shortage. Every mainline denomination in America suffers from the same dilemma. Denominations wrestle with the so-called problem of the empty pulpits, and there seems to be no relief in sight. The implication is that we have a numbers problem. That is, if we had sufficient numbers of pastors for those "empty pulpits," this dilemma would disappear.

I am convinced that a greater problem is the pulpits that appear to be filled but are, in fact, vacant because they lack not a warm body but the very same spirit that was in Joshua. We do not need more pastors. We need better pastors filled with Joshua's spirit. Much is made, too, of clergy burnout. It is a serious problem and will likely become increasingly so as the ratio of pastors to congregations continues to decline. I know about it firsthand. I also see it among some friends. However, I see more of what I call "Lazy Pastor Syndrome." There are too many pastors who will rust out long before they burn out simply because they lack the commitment to put in the hours and pour out the energy necessary to advance the Kingdom where they serve. No longer soaring eagles, they have become lifeless turkeys wandering aimlessly from day to day in a land of promise.

I once heard the late Bill Bright, founder of Campus Crusade for Christ, tell a story about an eagle that thought it was a barnyard chicken. Hence it spent its life walking around a barnyard, eating the grit and gravel below it. One day a beautiful eagle flew above it, soaring on wings directed by the wind. The bird looked up for a moment and said, "I wish I could soar like that, but I can't for I'm just a barnyard chicken." But he wasn't! He was an eagle, and he needed only to look again at who he was created to be and try his wings. That eagle reminds me of many pastors I meet. Theirs is not a problem of overwork but of low expectation. They do not expect much, nor do they have a burning desire for their churches to rise to new heights of greatness. As a result, not much happens there that is exciting. It is a problem that begins with attitude. Too many pas-

tors I know are retreating behind ecclesiastical committees, biding their
time until retirement or some "better opportunity" comes their way.
Theirs is no longer a call from God. It is a job and a chore. They fail to
realize that the best opportunity we have—indeed, the only opportunity
we have—is the one we have where we are today.

These "watchmen of uncertain trumpets" (see Ezek. 33:6-7) settle
for preaching that is dull, dreary, lifeless, and unexciting. It neither seeks
nor builds a spirit of enthusiasm (the word means "in-God-ism") among
the people to whom it is addressed. Hence it is no wonder that the number of people who experience a personal sense of calling under their ministries is virtually nonexistent. Others seem to be more interested in
building careers than building the congregations where they are right
now. The calling of the hour is for a new sense of calling—for pastors
who will view pastoral ministry not as a job but as an urgent response to
God's summons; for pastors full of Joshua's spirit, who are willing to stop
counting hours and seeking glory for themselves and give ministry their
best efforts. Our challenge is not clergy dropout but clergy cop-out!

My prayer as I write these words is that wherever they are read,
they will help ignite a new desire for excellence in pulpits and among
pastors. When that happens, however it happens, pastoral ministry will
be revived again and pastoral ranks will grow. It will only happen when
we as pastors recommit ourselves to reach higher than we are or have
been, that is, reach up for excellence. I find in my own ministry that it
begins each Sunday evening when I begin to zero in on my message for
the coming week. Having done most of my advance planning and research over the preceding months, now the challenge is to make sure
that the message I deliver to God's people next Sunday morning will be
better than the one I just delivered that morning, better than any I have
brought them before.

As Tom Peters and Nancy Austin remind us in _A Passion for Excellence: The Leadership Difference_, excellence begins with thinking big. It
grows out of a burning desire to do our best. It also demands a price and
is not for the faint of heart. To settle for less than giving our best should
really "bother us."[8]

How will that happen in your life and ministry? It will not happen
without prayer, and it will not occur without taking God's Word seriously. It calls for determination to rise above the ordinary, to keep going after others quit. Neither will it happen in the hearts of the people God
entrusts to my pastoral care until it happens in my heart. It can begin
today as we resolve to rise above what we have been and become more

like the pastors God made us to be. We must each personalize the psalmist's prayer, "Will you not revive us again, that your people may rejoice in you?" (Ps. 85:6). If we will inspire the church to excellence, we pastors must first reach for excellence in our own lives. Let us settle for nothing less.

WHEN GOOD ENOUGH SIMPLY ISN'T GOOD ENOUGH IN THE PEWS

Not long ago I asked a group of church leaders how many of them would allow threadbare, frazzled-edge carpet—like the one that for years covered the floor of their otherwise spectacular sanctuary—lie in their own homes. "How many of you," I quizzed them, "have carpet in this condition on the floors of your home?" No one answered. Next I asked, "How many of you have thrown away better carpet than this from your own homes?" Several raised their hands. Of the 20 or so people who heard my question, not one said such carpet would be acceptable in their homes. One elder, perhaps suspecting where my questions were leading them, protested my approach. "What would your wife say," I asked him, "if you were to bring this carpet home today and tell her you planned to install it in the living room?" "She wouldn't let either it or me in the door," he admitted. "Yet," I responded, "you and your fellow elders have apparently decided that carpet like this is good enough for God's house!" He may not have liked my comeback, but I think he began to get the point.

All too often as I visit around churches, unchallenged church members and leaders treat God's house as a hand-me-down center for furniture, office equipment, and other items that they have decided are no longer good enough for their business offices or homes. Items that are no longer in good working order or that have been replaced by much improved new models in our business offices are often given to the church of Jesus Christ. Worse still, they are accepted with at least feigned gratitude by mealymouthed pastors and church leaders. The spirit of Ananias and Sapphira is still alive in many places in the church of the new millennium! Something is seriously wrong when we try to palm off anything less than our absolute best to the One who gave His best for us on Calvary and "called us by His own glory and excellence" (2 Pet. 1:3, NASB). Whatever happened to "Give of your best to the Master"? The issue is excellence. Anything short of excellence is mediocrity or worse.

It is not the pastors alone who must work to bring about a renewed spirit of excellence in the church. The laity, too, must rise to newness of spirit if we are to know revival. Without a determination to reach for excellence from the pews, any attempt to do so from the pulpits will likely be short-lived. The laity must come to see and acknowledge that the church is simply losing its impact in the world.

"Moses' hands were heavy. Then they took a stone and put it under him, and he sat on it; and Aaron and Hur supported his hands, one on one side and one on the other. Thus his hands were steady until the sun set" (Exod. 17:12, NASB). God used Dale Bogard to save my ministry, perhaps even to save my life. At a critical point, when it looked as though the enemies of renewal at our church might succeed in ending my ministry, Dale came to my office unannounced one evening when I was especially low. He said, "I'm here for one reason, and it's to hold up your arms." He remembered how Aaron and Hur stood by Moses' side and held up his arms to bring about the victory against Amalek. Dale decided God was calling him to do the same thing for his pastor. I can never repay him for the inspiration his presence and words brought me at a time of spiritual lowness that bordered on defeat. It was a critical moment, but God, through Dale, let me know that I was not alone in the battle and that I was loved.

When love comes into the picture, especially in times of discouragement, it presents to the world an indisputable mark of a true follower of Jesus Christ and a force that will never be overcome. As a result, a special bond developed between Dale and me. There is nothing I would not do for him, and there is nothing he could say that would offend me. In the months and years that followed, Dale has come to me with suggestions and corrections many times. Because of him, I am a better pastor and a better man. He has helped me in the pursuit of excellence. I am convinced that every pastor needs a Dale Bogard in his or her life— to bring a word of encouragement or inspiration, offer support in prayer, or walk beside the pastor in troubled times. I am convinced that had Dale not come that evening and offered to hold up my arms, I would have become totally discouraged and lost the battle. Furthermore, I am convinced that every pastor will benefit from the support and loving direction of the laity.

You do understand, don't you, that God has given the church and its pastors an overwhelming assignment for this new millennium? We are called to take the redemptive word of Christ's Cross to a new generation. It is a generation that does not always welcome God's Word, one that sees a lot of reasons to have little or nothing to do with the church as it knows it. No pastor can accomplish this task alone. Pastors need the Holy Spirit to inspire, lead, and empower them. That will happen often through laypeople who are ready to stand with their pastors in this battle for the hearts and souls of people both inside and outside the church. What the church needs now are not more and more people but better and better people. Jesus Christ called out 12 to walk especially close to Him. One of those was a dud, but through the other 11 and their spiritual offspring, God started a fire in Jerusalem that has never gone out and never will. Our call as pastors and laity alike is to burn the flame ever brighter by committing ourselves to better serving Him in His church every single day for the rest of our lives. What the church needs is a determined pursuit of excellence, and it will come nearer to finding it when you resolve that you will reach higher to do your best.

What can you as a layperson do to inspire excellence in your church and in your pastor? What follows are some suggestions:

- Come to see unity as a special gift from God.
- Recognize the calling of your pastor as sacred—a treasure to be valued—and challenge your pastor to lead you to new heights with Christ.
- Ask yourself what obstacles to excellence exist in your church, and work with all your heart to help your pastor overcome them.
- Commit yourself to affirming your pastor when he or she does something worthy of praise, and gently correct him or her when you feel he or she is not delivering his or her best for Christ.
- Make sure that ample provision of time and financial support is made for your pastor to have an opportunity for rest and spiritual refreshment, and make sure that the pastor takes full advantage of such opportunities.
- Determine that you will speak only well of the pastor and that where necessary, you will do all in your power to quench detractors, gossips, and unfair critics.
- Resolve with God's help that you will personally reach for new levels of excellence in your own spiritual life.
- Steward your life in such a way as to allow time each day to pray for a renewed spirit of excellence to enter your church, and resolve with God's help to do everything in your power to make it come to pass.

"Just as you excel in everything—in faith, in speech, in knowledge, in complete earnestness and in your love for us—see that you also excel in this grace of giving" (2 Cor. 8:7). Let us be careful not to quickly jump only to the financial aspects of these words. To be sure, they speak to Christian stewardship, but they are far more than that alone. The

Corinthian Christians excelled in all things, whether faith, speech (preaching), learning, sincerity, and love. Theirs was a case of excellence in all things. Whether clergy or lay leader, the reality is that there are no good alternatives to excellence. Either a thing is excellent or it is mediocre, second best, substandard, or good enough. But good enough is not good enough for the One who gave His all for us that we might live life in abundance. Whether clergy or laity, we are challenged throughout Scripture to go above and beyond and do our utmost for God's kingdom. There is no higher calling than the relentless pursuit of excellence for Christ.

Notes

1. *Leadership*, Vol. 4, no. 3.

2. Tim Hansel, *Holy Sweat* (Waco, Tex.: Word, 1987), 111.

3. *Our Daily Bread*, published by RBC Ministries—Grand Rapids, MI 49555, 25 January 1993.

4. Rick Kogan, "Good Days for Paul Harvey," *Chicago Tribune Magazine*, 4 August 2002, 10.

5. Adapted from Paul Harvey News broadcast, 22 November 1995.

6. Ted W. Engstrom, *The Pursuit of Excellence* (Grand Rapids: Zondervan, 1982), 24.

7. *New York Times On-line* edition, 13 October 2003.

8. Tom Peters and Nancy Austin, *A Passion for Excellence: The Leadership Difference* (New York: Random House, 1985), 414-15.

Darius Salter, Ph.D., is professor of Christian preaching and pastoral theology at Nazarene Theological Seminary in Kansas City. For eight years he served as chairman of the Pastoral Studies Department at Western Evangelical Seminary in Portland, Oregon. He was the executive director of the Christian Holiness Association, an interdenominational fellowship consisting of 17 denominations, 50 colleges and universities, and two missionary organizations, from 1979 to 1986. He is a sought-after speaker in spiritual life campaigns and camp meetings. His published works include *What Really Matters in Ministry: Profiling Pastoral Success in Flourishing Churches, American Evangelism: Its Theology and Practice, Prophetical-Priestly Words: Biblical Identity for the 21st Century Pastor,* and *America's Bishop: The Life of Francis Asbury.* Dr. Salter and his wife, Brenda, have four daughters: Heather, Heidi, Tabitha, and Ashley. The Salters reside in Lake Winnebago, Missouri.

5

Engaging God in Worship
Four Delicate Tensions
Darius Salter

WORSHIP IS NOT A PROBLEM TO BE SOLVED. It is not a formula to be routinized. Worship is elusive. It is elusive because God is elusive. As the male lover in the Song of Solomon, God knocks at the door, but when the door is opened, He is not there. He woos us into the street, but the morning fog obscures His location. Worship eludes us, because the "us" consists of people—people distracted by credit card debt, imperfect relationships, and the angst that grips all of us. Self-gratification clouds the beatific vision; a vision that often can only be clarified by some kind of crisis, such as disease, death, or divorce.

Worship is not an either-or experience. We worship in varying degrees. Rarely do I go to church and have a "sixth-chapter" Isaiah experience or anything close to it. On the other hand, rarely do I go to church and not have God engage me in some sort of way. The Holy Spirit reminds me of God's holiness and my failures. A vision of both is critical to worship. Seldom do I attend a corporate worship service that I do not receive grace through the sacraments represented and offered by the gospel community. I engage God in varying dimensions and intensities.

As I write this, I am sitting at a picnic table canopied by oak trees and a clear blue sky. I am at peace with my surroundings and the God who created them. What has brought me here is a curious, 200-year-old institution called a camp meeting. I am the featured speaker. Last Sunday morning's service consisted of gospel songs, testimonies from the congregants, extemporaneous prayers, a lengthy appeal for money, a boisterous sermon, and an invitation to make a definitive decision about one's relationship with God. All of this may seem a bit hokey to millions of Christians around the world who, at the very same time, were processing into churches, lighting candles, reading lectionary-assigned scriptures, preaching from carefully prepared manuscripts, and celebrating the Eucharist with sophisticated rituals. To ask, "Who truly worships?" in these contrasting settings brings us to my first observation about Christian corporate worship at the beginning of the third millennium. We are paying too much attention to the "how" of worship rather than the God who is to be worshiped.

God demands worship be defined and characterized by "spirit" and "truth." Worship is affective and cognitive, emotional and intellectual, psychological and doctrinal, subjective and objective. Augustine stated, "What one does not know, he cannot love, and what one does not love, he cannot know." Knowing and loving are inextricably bound together.

The knowing and the loving are contextualized by time and culture. Hanging in the dining hall of the camp meeting in which I am now participating is a picture of the attendees at the camp meeting of 1925. I stare into their faces, faces hardened by an agrarian life consisting of heat and flies, dust and humidity, and all the other parasitical elements that rob life of its pleasure. Certainly the oppressive August heat, the long wagon ride, the lack of sanitary facilities, and the crowded sleeping tent must have distracted from worship. Focus on God pleads for liberation from minuscule distractions and aggravations or at least for transcendence over them.

Whether creature comforts and technical innovations enable us to engage God leads to a second simple observation: worship for a good many of us should focus far less on the outer accoutrements and amenities and far more on our motives and values. A certain family traveling to a camp meeting a century ago spent several days carefully loading their wagon for the long trip and ensuing two-week stay. Along the way, the lantern caught the hay on fire and the entire wagon and its contents were consumed. Rather than go back home, the family walked the rest of the way to the camp meeting, where they were befriended and supplied by fellow campers. It may have been at that camp meeting that they engaged God as never before.

The above anecdotal musing leads to a third personal viewpoint. There are no worship tools and devices that ensure the presence of God. Yes, I do believe in the *ex opere operato* of worship acts (the grace-conveying capability of the rites by themselves) that transcends both intention and understanding, because the sacraments are predicated on divine generosity rather than human intent. E. Schillebeeckx states that "the sacraments confer grace *ex opere operato*. . . . Put negatively, the significance of sacramental efficacy *ex opere operato* is that the bestowal of grace is not dependent upon the sanctity of ministry, nor does the faith of the recipient put any obligation on grace; Christ remains free, sovereign, and independent with regard to any human merit whatsoever."[1]

Schillebeeckx's assessment resonates with my Wesleyan theology. The doctrine of prevenient grace teaches me that God is present before, during, and after participation in corporate worship in ways that are beyond both my intention and perception. In the words of someone else, "God is sneaky." He creeps up on us when we least expect it and at times seems absent when we have done everything humanly possible to ensure His presence.

Yet conditions and contingencies exist that are vital to faithfully connecting with God. The very nature of corporate worship is that grace flows more freely both to and between reconciled persons attempting with the Holy Spirit's help to "love mercy, do justly, and walk humbly with their God." Schillebeeckx states that "all the faithful are concerned in a sacramental act of faith of the Church as a public confession of their own faith. . . . The holiness of the church, which together with the holiness of Christ is here sacramentalized, is not the holiness of some abstract entity, but rather of all those who belong in grace to this church."[2] In other words, a people who internalize Christ, becoming tabernacles of the living God, become sacraments to one another.

Corporate worship is predicated primarily on grace that flows from God and secondarily, but extremely vital, grace that flows to and from one another. Regarding the Early Church, Acts 4:34 records that "neither was there any among them that lacked" (KJV). To the extent that this does not characterize upwardly mobile, privatized Americans, to that extent worship eludes those of us who neatly and impatiently settle in for our "one hour per Sunday" God engagement. Knowing that I am selfish, materialistic, competitive, and independent stalks me as I enter and exit God's house. The problem is with me, not with the God who has redeemed me.

True worship is both fulfilling and troublesome. It is tricky business, as Uzziah and the sons of both Aaron and Eli discovered. Telling someone else how to worship smacks of committing the gross sins of hypocrisy and ethnocentricity. You would learn far more by visiting a Christian community in the Ukraine or Uganda than by reading a chapter titled "Engaging God in Worship." However, I am going to suggest four worship tensions or polarities that must be delicately negotiated if corporate worship is going to bring God the pleasure He is due because He is God.

I. FORMAL VS. INFORMAL

Much of American Evangelical worship inherits from the Reformation, and specifically Puritanism, worship that is not liturgically ordered by either national or ecclesiastical authority. This does not mean that Evangelical worship is formless. It simply means that it chooses not to use (often out of ignorance) prayers, collects, confessions, and creeds found in the *Book of Common Prayer* or even more ancient sources. But form is no less cherished by most American churches than it was by Thomas Cranmer, the author of the *Book of Common Prayer*. Any freshly minted seminary graduate will receive less than an enthusiastic response when he or she includes the "Collect for Purity" as part of the worship service, at least within the first year of his or her ministry. This new innovation (new as far as the congregation is concerned) would preempt or disturb the ritual of the church, which has been in place for years.

I remind seminary students that they do not have to reinvent the wheel every time they prepare a worship service. The *Book of Common Prayer* accompanied by more recent sources (Wesley's Covenant Service) enriches worship with deep theological and biblical roots. The carefully worded ascriptions and confessions are gifts handed down from one generation to another throughout the 2,000-year history of the Church. Thomas Oden charges the Church with a moral accountability to give heed to a worship tradition that has been carefully honed throughout the centuries. "For we speak to and for a community that is heir of the prophets, apostles, and martyrs, the grace-laden heritage of centuries of costly confessing faith."[3]

But frankly, some seminary graduates will not be able to employ these historical forms without emptying out either a country or inner-city church. Rather than using a "push comes to shove" approach, a pastor would do far better to pray that God would anoint the forms already in place. Corporate worship is glorifying God through the practice of ritual by two or more persons in unison. To engage God, a worship form will need to center on Christ by the power of the Holy Spirit. To facilitate worship, a form will have to freshly engage the living Christ. Thus any form, both ancient and modern, can become perfunctory. An altar call at a camp meeting can be as routinized and ritualized as any complex rite practiced during the Middle Ages.

If form, sophisticated or simple, does not enable an encounter with the *tremendum* (fearsome power) and *mysterium* (incomprehensibleness) of God, it will not engage God. Without the corporal and sensual reality of form as a means, a person cannot engage the numinous (holy divine presence). The seen is the primary avenue through which we can worship the unseen God. In the words of Schillebeeckx, "God always offers us the kingdom of heaven in an earthly guise."[4] Thus at the heart of all worship is incarnation, the Logos becoming flesh so that we may see God. The temporal transports us to the eternal by physical acts consecrated by the church and sanctified by the Holy Spirit.

How this transportation takes place is a mystery, and once it ceases to be a mystery and becomes a rational construct that attempts to ensure God's presence, it ceases to be worship. This is not to say that ritual needs to be deconceptualized. Quite the contrary, according to Rudolph Otto, Christianity possesses conceptions about God that are superior to its "sister religions." Otto critically points out that "by being steeped in and saturated with rational elements it is guarded from sinking into fanaticism or mere mysticality, or at least from persisting in these, and is qualified to become a religion for all civilized humanity."[5] But as Otto argues, rationalization of the rational is one of the chief impediments to true worship. Any form of the most Episcopal gatherings or most backwoodsy Pentecostal Church in Eastern Kentucky becomes idolatrous if it loses its wonder and amazement because it ceases to reveal the God who cannot be grasped by any particular form or formula. The ineffability of God's holiness eludes rational containment. Sooner or later God cuts loose from every form and abandons it, at least for a time. God despises containment. Otto claims that the God of the Bible "who admits access to himself and intimacy with himself is not a mere matter of course; it is a grace beyond our power to apprehend, a prodigious paradox."[6]

The forms of worship must be considered as means of grace and not merit. Perceiving that God will meet with us because our forms are better than the forms used by other groups is pride coming before the fall. In God's assessment, sincerity of the ritual always counts for more than the form of the ritual. The forms must constantly evidence that "the sacrifices of God are a broken spirit: a broken and a contrite heart, O God, thou wilt not despise" (Ps. 51:17, KJV). Both underconfidence and overconfidence are two dangers in worship ritual. David Peterson stresses this dialectic when he states, "Formality may be the expression of a very narrow and inadequate view of worship; and informality may be an excuse for lack of preparation or any serious attempt to engage collectively with God."[7]

II. Preparation vs. Spontaneity

Corporate worship requires preparation. Preparation involves far more than scheduling the activities of an hour-long gathering of people.

Preparation for corporate worship is foremost an anointed waiting before God of mind and spirit. It is not a prayer asking God to meet us in some certain special way when we arrive at the place of worship (the zap theory?). Portable tabernacles (those bearing Christ within) approach the place of worship with the promise that Christ will be in the midst of His people. He has promised to be present when two or three are gathered in His name. For this we must be ready.

Thus I favor the Jewish ordering of Sabbath time rather than the American Evangelical ordering of Sunday. First, I would argue that the Christian Sabbath should be from 6 P.M. Saturday to 6 P.M. Sunday. Saturday evening would be a time of family worship; this would preempt the details that normally bog us down and the entertainment that often consumes us. The transition from secular to sacred cannot take place by stepping through the door of a church on Sunday at 10:55 A.M.

Now to be clear, I do believe that in a sense all of life is sacred and, in the words of Elton Trueblood, that we live in a "sacramental world." So whenever Christians gather, whatever day of the week, God has promised to be present. And just as important I also believe that "every home should become a Christian society and every common meal a sacramental experience."[8] Thus a congruency exists between the sacrament of living Monday through Saturday and the worship that takes place on Sunday morning. But at the same time, a qualitative difference exists between the Christian Sabbath and the rest of the week. The Sabbath is set aside for an intentional God encounter. God offers the Sabbath rest to save us from our restlessness—the acquisitiveness, greed, and accumulation of things that tears and wears at all of us. In this way Sunday assumes a uniquely sacred function that beckons us to be prepared.

The preparation the Christian makes for Sunday's God encounter needs to be open-ended. Fixing high noon on Sunday as the closing time for meeting with God is a failure to allow God to be God. He can never be perfectly read, and He is often (always?) unpredictable. Do we need to meditate on Christ's words to Nicodemas? "The wind blows where it wishes, and you hear the sound of it, but do not know where it comes from and where it goes. So is everyone who is born of the Spirit" (John 3:8, NKJV).

I do not believe that every worship service should be a Pentecost revisited. Pentecost is not the norm of Christian worship because God cannot be contained in a norm. But having an openness to the extraordinariness of Pentecost needs to be the norm of preparation. The dynamic of the numinous sanctifies sincere preparation so that the ensuing combination of people, ritual, and setting becomes a unique, one-time-only event. In other words, when my preparation is surrendered to God, God will take circumstances, problems, people, sacred acts, sacred objects, and sacred words and blend them together in ways I could not envision. Momentous and monumental destiny is the exclamation mark over every gathering of God's people!

As a pastor my perception of what needs to happen will be interrupted, interpreted, or transcended by God's perfect plan, which always needs to superintend my shortsightedness. But this does not mean I have any more license to slack off in my preparation than do those sitting in the pews. The *mysterium* is never equated with an off-the-cuff, slovenly, impulsive, carelessly prepared worship script. Doing less than my best for God results in condemnation of both people and pastor. The transition from Old Testament law to New Testament grace is not an invitation to profane God's name by a haphazard entrance into His presence.

III. Order vs. Charisms

The most complete description and instruction for worship in the New Testament is 1 Cor. 14. In verse 26, we are told, "When you assemble, each one has a psalm, has a teaching, has a revelation, has a tongue, has an interpretation" (NASB). In other words, each attendee is to bring a gift (*charism*) to a Christian assembly. Yet in verse 40, we are exhorted that everything should "be done properly and in an orderly manner" (NASB). Throughout the centuries the Christian Church has agonizingly tried to reconcile these two parameters. We have sound historical evidence that by the middle of the second century the Church had opted for order. Justin Martyr gives a description of second-century worship that admits little of "transrational" or charismatic eruptions. Is Hans Kung correct when he charges the Church with regressing to Jewish offices rather than charismatic leadership?[9] Had the Church within the first 100 years of its existence traded Spirit-led leadership and worship for institutional predictability?

Order as opposed to freedom was a particular problem for early American Methodism. The children of Anglicanism encountered prostration, jerking, jumping, and shouting—the kind of spiritual confusion that seems far removed from the intelligible and accountable behavior for which Paul argues. Yet it was in the context of such irrational worship that Methodism enjoyed its greatest harvest, growing seven times as fast as the U.S. population between 1800 and 1810.

With the Methodists of 200 years ago we share two nonnegotiable staples: life and edification. Life consists not of emotionalism but emotion. Emotionalism is emotion for emotion's sake, a subjective feeling sought for its own thrill rather than for the glory of God. But good worship is no more void of emotion than is good sex. Psychosexual intimacy should be accompanied by ecstatic joy, the delight of being able to give oneself unreservedly to another. Laughter, tears, glee, and excitement may not be constants of worship, but the constant absence of them spells death rather than life. Worship is like eros in that it "infuses wishes, cravings, and longings in personal liking, friendship and love in song and poetry and imaginative creation in general."[10] Eros and worship are responsible for most of the art that has ever been created. No art is detached from emotion. Emotionless worship is a contradiction in terms.

Edification, as the apostle Paul emphasized, is a critical evaluation for propriety in worship. Corporate Christian worship, if it is truly Christian, blasts American individualism with a concern for the welfare of one another. Edification takes the form of a holy hush or a holy holler, acted word or spoken word, handshake or hug. These acts are essential to Christian worship. There is no way to encounter the God of corporate worship without encountering the God who resides in one another. We edify, build up, each other by Spirit-led responses that are as varied and spontaneous as the need of the moment. An essential preparation for corporate worship is the petition that God will enable us to be couriers of grace to one another. To truly celebrate the redemption of Christ is to become each other's redemptive agent.

Every church needs to ponder Kung's directive that "the true charism is not simply a miracle; it is something in the service of the community; giving a sense of responsibility towards the community and the desire to edify and benefit it. Charism is directly connected with the community."[11] Every act of worship has to be encompassed with the question, "How does this benefit my brother and sister?" An act of redemption is any interpersonal sacrament that enables the other to become a better person, that is, to enter into God's definition of blessedness. Such signs of care, love, and concern are both rational and "transrational." A word of encouragement provides courage; a holy dance communicates that you, too, are free to dance.

God is community—a trinity. Community is as unpredictable as my relationship with my wife. There is an aspect of worship that needs to be as uncalculated as any love affair. The Trinity is a sociality of being, a sociality that is extended to God's children, those made in His image. Irreconcilability between the children of God equates to not being reconciled to God. Nothing brings more glory to God than when we approximate the fellowship that the persons of the Trinity have among themselves. We fulfill the prayer Christ prayed for us when we gather together—"the love wherewith Thou didst love me may be in them, and I in them" (John 17:26, NASB). God's gifts *(charisms)* bring life to worship, love and joy flowing within the Body. True worship always takes place at the intersection of order and surprise.

IV. NURTURE VS. TRANSFORMATION

I recently asked the pastor of a large church, "How did you find Christ or how did He find you?" (The latter question is more theologically correct than the former.) He answered, "Well, it was enough to make me believe in predestination. I was 18 years old and had already been in jail for a felony. I was addicted to alcohol, and if drugs had been available, I would have been addicted to them. I was from an extremely dysfunctional home. My alcoholic father was abusive. I remember the day in the fifth grade when my mother came to school to exit me and my siblings so we could move to another state in order to escape my father. At age 18, some friends invited me to the Church of the Nazarene. I went in order to get them off my back, thinking it would be the first and last time I attended. I did not understand a single thing that took place in the worship service. Neither did I understand anything the preacher said in the sermon. At the end of his sermon, the pastor gave an invitation. I just stood there with little to no comprehension of what was going on. The preacher, noting my bewilderment, came down from the pulpit and asked, 'Young man, would you like to give your life to Christ?' I answered, 'I reckon.' I knelt at the altar for one hour, and at 1 P.M. I walked out a changed man."

This man answered a call to preach and has now been pastoring for 35 years. Wesleyan theology has historically been characterized by a radical optimism of grace that accents "now" theology. An outlandish sinner responded to the invitation of a Methodist itinerant 200 years ago, "You don't mean that God would forgive so many sins in so short a time?" At the heart of John Wesley's and Francis Asbury's preaching was the exhortation to believe now and to expect now. Nineteenth-century Methodists and, until recently, the ensuing Holiness Movement have believed and practiced that the optimum opportunity for transformation, justification, and entire sanctification has been within the gathered community.

Gently nudging the crisis model of worship aside over the last several years (particularly in the Holiness Movement) has been a nurturing or spiritual formation model of worship. This spiritual paradigm has largely abandoned the expectation that people can and will be radically transformed within the context of worship. In other words, an evangelistic model of worship that offers immediate deliverance from sin and guilt has been displaced by less traumatic and more gradual expectations for spiritual transformation.

A crisis model of worship has not been without its problems. Evangelists have manipulated, musicians have agitated, exaggerated stories have frightened, and preachers have masterly produced guilt. This has led to the conviction that anything observed in a worship service can be produced psychologically. Clarke Garrett is at least partially correct when he states that "spirit possession and hysteria become two names for the same things—a spectacular body language for expressing convictions too profound, too painful or too dangerous to be expressed verbally."[12]

The goal of worship is not evangelistic production and certainly not paroxysms of emotion. Worship is not teleological; that is, it is not for the purpose of producing that which can be seen, felt, or heard. True worship is not measurable. Not every service should end with an altar call. But every gathering of God's people that includes a proclamation of both the written and Living Word issues an invitation to both saint and sinner. The invitation may be stated or unstated, overt or covert, implicit or explicit, corporate or individual. In at least some worship gatherings, someone if not everyone ought to say with Isaiah, "Woe is me, for I am ruined! Because I am a man of unclean lips, and I live among a people of unclean lips; for my eyes have seen the King, the LORD of hosts" (Isa. 6:5, NASB). (Was Isaiah alone in the Temple?) Encounter with God always translates to encounter with oneself.

Over the last 25 years, the spiritual formation movement has reintroduced the Body of Christ to many spiritual disciplines that have historically been at the heart of vital Christianity: spiritual direction, scripture meditation, small groups, fasting, confession, and the celebration of the Eucharist when God's people come together. I am optimistic that both the evangelistic and nurturing models can learn from and contribute to one another. Authentic worship always awakens us to our needs and to the needs of the world around us. Even more importantly, the God that I engage in worship offers hope that things can be different for both me and the world I am called to serve. The grace of corporate worship shifts the balance between good and evil within me so that I might enhance the good in a world that is characterized by lostness.

My prayer is not primarily that worship will change me. My prayer is that both I and those with whom I worship will see the holy God of glory. When this happens, we leave God's house different than when we came.

CONCLUSION

Geoffrey Wainwright reminds us that *lex orandi* informs *lex crendendi*; that is, the law of prayer (worship) informs the law of belief (doctrine and creed).[13] As a person attends one worship service after another throughout life, an understanding and identification of God evolves. The god that one engages may be the god of America, the god of the Republican party, the god of materialism, or the god of competition. Hopefully not! It is the prophet/priest's job to enable persons within his or her sphere of ministry to discover the God who is revealed in Scripture. When that happens, people will become more Christian. This is the yardstick that distinguishes between engaging the God of creation or the god of entertainment that the popular culture demands. The ultimate job of any liturgist is getting God right.

But getting God right has no finale in this life. Knowing that "we see through a glass darkly" bathes us with humility. Trueblood reminds us that "it is only honest to admit that it is difficult, and probably impossible, to bring together in one pattern all of the features which are patent means of worship to all people."[14] A security of identity and a genuine openness to the diverse forms and rituals of other denominational and cultural communities may be the most delicate dialectic of all tensions within Christian corporate worship.

Notes

1. E. Schillebeeckx, *Christ the Sacrament of the Encounter with God* (Franklin, Wis.: Sheed and Ward, 1999), 69-70.

2. Ibid., 67-68.

3. Thomas Oden, *Pastoral Theology: Essentials of Ministry* (San Francisco: Harper and Row, Publishers, 1983), 94.

4. Schillebeeckx, *Christ the Sacrament*, 42.

5. Rudolph Otto, *The Idea of the Holy* (New York: Oxford University Press, 1958), 141.

6. Ibid., 56.

7. David Peterson, *Engaging with God* (Downers Grove, Ill.: InterVarsity Press, 1992), 160.

8. Elton Trueblood, *A People Called Quakers* (New York: Harper and Row, 1966), 146.

9. Hans Kung, *The Church* (Garden City, N.Y.: Image Books, 1976), 495-546.

10. Otto, *Idea of the Holy*, 46.

11. Kung, *The Church*, 240.

12. Clarke Garrett, *Spirit Possession and Popular Religion* (Baltimore: Johns Hopkins, 1987), 4.

13. Geoffrey Wainwright, *The Praise of God in Worship, Doctrine, and Life* (New York: Oxford University Press, 1980), 218-83.

14. Trueblood, *A People Called Quakers*, 96.

H. B. London Jr. has served for more than a decade as vice president of ministry outreach/pastoral ministries at Focus on the Family, Colorado Springs. Prior to his current assignment as a "pastor to pastors," he served congregations as a shepherd-leader for 31 years. He is author of *Refresh, Renew, Revive* and coauthor (with Neil Wiseman) of *The Heart of a Great Pastor* and *They Call Me Pastor*, and most recently *For Kids' Sake—Winning the Tug-of-War for Future Generations.* Pastor London and his wife, Beverley, have two married sons and four grandchildren.

Neil B. Wiseman, after 20 years of ministry as a parish pastor, served as academic dean and professor of pastoral development at Nazarene Bible College, Colorado Springs. His other development efforts for ministers include founding and leading Preaching Today, the Minister's Tape Club, Small Church Institute, and *GROW* magazine. He holds degrees from Olivet Nazarene University, Nazarene Theological Seminary, and Vanderbilt Divinity School. Neil and his wife, Bonnie, have two married sons and three grandchildren.

6

A Fresh Encounter with God

H. B. London Jr. and Neil B. Wiseman

Father, send revival and renewal to my soul and church. Invigorate, rejuvenate, and revitalize every phase of my ministry. Help me live by the reality that I can do nothing without You. Amen.

"It's Me, It's Me, O Lord"

"A few members of any church must get thoroughly right with God," was evangelist Dr. R. A. Torrey's first rule for revival. However, if a pastor is serious about renewal in his or her ministry and church, the rule must be personalized with the pastor's name and address and zip code.

Then the rule reads, "Let (insert your name) get thoroughly right with God as a first step of revival." To reinforce the revival rule we sing, "It's me, it's me, O Lord, standing in the need of prayer."

The supernatural power of personal revival is illustrated in the following testimony that I (H. B.) shared at a pastors' conference.

Pastor Shares His Need of Renewal

A life-changing renewal came to me after I had been a pastor for 15 years in Salem, Oregon. I was a pastor of a spiritually vibrant church, but I still saw myself as a phony. I went through the right motions without the right motives. I saw myself accomplishing about what anyone could do if given the same opportunities. My success, however, was not comfort enough. I needed healing, revival.

One night in a dark, silent church when no one was present, I fell across the altar in a mood of spiritual desperation. I began to pray the most humiliating prayer you could imagine.

I prayed, "O God, I want out of this. I want out of the ministry. I'm not worthy of this church. I'm artificial and a playactor. You need to get me out of this. I would appreciate it if You could get me out gracefully. But if it is not graceful, that's OK too. I just can't go on with this pain inside."

At that point, I humbled myself. I admitted to God that I was not authentic. I acknowledged that I was inadequate. I confessed that I was an unworthy vessel, full of cracks and holes. I admitted that I was running on spiritual empty.

At that moment, the presence of Christ came over me with empowerment and meaning. The Lord seemed to say in that moment, "Now I can use you." The results of that encounter with the Lord changed my whole life. It revolutionized my ministry.

Personalizing Torrey's rule may seem a bit uncomfortable at first. But spiritual development never works for "them" before it starts with "us"—for "me." Like so many things in ministry, revival is a matter of leadership, priority, and visibility.

From what you know about God and about how churches function, you know that few congregations will become spiritual powerhouses until their pastors first experience a fresh personal encounter with God. Consequently, the first step for authentic revival is personal renewal of the pastor at any cost.

The second step follows the first automatically. A genuine spiritual awakening causes a pastor to feel a holy dissatisfaction with things as they are. Thousands of ministers who become fed up must speak up in kindly but unmistakable ways about what needs to be changed.

Our legitimate discontent centers around playing church, coddling emotional infants, worrying about personal security, preaching arid doctrinal scholasticism, baby-sitting trivia, being controlled by spiritual pygmies, and living by savage schedules that leave no time for prayer, study, or outreach.

It's time to face the fact that the nation's moral malaise and the Church's naval-gazing apathy are sobering, serious spiritual issues. It's time to seek reality in knowing God, to fast, to receive God's perspective, and to insist upon authenticity in ourselves and in church leaders above and below us. It's time to get serious about holy living so that it becomes a personal and congregational obsession.

It's time to move beyond puny image building about small successes to accomplishing truly supernatural exploits for God—the kind that transform individuals and revolutionize society. It's time to rally all the church's facilities, finances, and personnel to win the war against evil and [godlessness].

For such a revival, we must pray Habakkuk's prayer for ourselves, our assignments, our denominations, our colleges, and our publishing houses, "O Lord, revive Thy work!" And we must march and sing:

> O Breath of Life, come sweeping through us;
> Revive Thy Church with life and power.
> O Breath of Life, come, cleanse, renew us;
> And fit Thy Church to meet this hour.[1]

MAKE *REVIVAL* A USER-FRIENDLY WORD

Revivals have a bad reputation in many places. Because a spurt of religious enthusiasm soon plays out, it is argued that planned and calendared revivals accomplish little. The conclusion seems overly jaded, however, when you consider that some renewal is better than none. A Methodist bishop said in a conversation where revival meetings were being criticized, "I agree that revivals are often ineffective, but that's how I got into the Kingdom."

The revival we need will take us back to the basics of faith and re-activate a no-reservations commitment to the cause of Christ. Such a revival will require us to humble our souls before God, to question our ego, and to get serious about personal righteousness. Such a revival will stimulate fresh love and soul-stretching adoration for Christ and will energize selfless service to God and neighbor.

Such a contagious revival will make the life of God satisfying, joyful, and fun again. And it will anoint our preaching with a holy contagion so we are able to make the gospel inviting and invigorating to a broken world.

Norman Vincent Peale paints a clear picture of the kind of revival we seek when he described his father's ministry as a revivalist, "What he [Peale's father] wanted was in-depth life-change in which not only emotion but the mind combined in a commitment bringing spiritual growth and lifelong Christian discipleship."[2]

That's real revival—an in-depth, life-changing commitment involving the emotions and mind that makes believers in our churches and we ourselves spiritually different and growing for a lifetime.

Look Beyond the Wrappings

More slick substitutes, maneuvering manipulation, or extreme emotionalism is not what we desire from revivals out of the past. Rather, it is the God of revival and renewal we seek.

Like stories from our childhood, it's fun to retell revival experiences from our past. I remember an evangelist who displayed an open casket with a mirror in place of a corpse at the front of the church. I recall singing 34 verses of "Just as I Am." In college years, I remember being tricked into admitting in public that I had not surrendered to Christ.

In my mind, I can still see eccentric evangelists out of the past with big cars, garish ties, giant Bibles, and flashy suits. Those itinerants sometimes sold study Bibles, records, books, or ceramic eagles to help them make a living. But these are just the wrappings. There is so much more to real revival.

Let's try looking past the externals to the essential. What is the essential nature of revival? What is the driving force for authentic revival?

For real revival to take place, God wants a minister and a church to thoroughly examine their relationship to Christ and to continually evaluate ministry in light of Kingdom priorities. Depth and obedience are to replace shallowness and playacting. God intends for revival to impact the heart of a pastor and the heart of a congregation.

For an individual, such a renewing welcomes God into the citadel of the soul. It joyously allows a loving Father to forgive outward sin and remedy inner corruption. Genuine revival makes us willing to turn from sin, rebellion, and disobedience. Genuine renewal requires humbling oneself, seeking God's face, turning from wicked ways, and changing in any way He suggests. Real revival helps us make the wonderful trade of giving up embarrassing self-sovereignty to receive God's guidance, grace, and will.

Follow Scriptural Directions

From Genesis to Revelation, the Bible is a book about reality and renewal and starting again. It encourages us to eagerly hope for revival, and it commands us to earnestly seek revival. We are to yearn for renewal as if it all comes from God. At the same time, we are to seek renewal as if its coming depends completely on us.

Scripture teaches that revival is more than a desirable wish or an idealized spiritual state of being. Rather, genuine revival is a revitalized faith God wants us to enjoy, a supernatural new vision for every church, and a favor we give ourselves.

Consider these scriptural directives for seeking authentic revival and for kindling genuine renewal.

Peter proclaims the necessity. At Pentecost, Peter proclaimed revival ingredients, "Repent, then, and turn to God, so that your sins may be wiped out, that times of refreshing may come from the Lord, and that he may send the Christ, who has been appointed for you— even Jesus" (Acts 3:19-20). _Jesus explains the source of revival._ Even after two centuries have passed, Jesus' immortal words at the Feast of Tabernacles still call the Church to authentic renewal, "If anyone is thirsty, let him come to me and drink. Whoever believes in me, as the Scripture has said, streams of living water will flow from within him" (John 7:37-38).

Revival impacts a nation. Scripture teaches a connection between a genuine revival of God's people and the spiritual salvaging of a nation. In the events surrounding the dedication of the Temple, this connection between the people of God and their nation appears at least twice.

Solomon prayed earnestly for God to honor their worship in the new location with His presence: "When your people Israel have been defeated by an enemy because they have sinned against you and when they turn back and confess your name, praying and making supplication before you in this temple, then hear from heaven and forgive the sin of your people Israel and bring them back to the land you gave to them and their fathers" (2 Chron. 6:24-25).

Note the relationship of the land to Israel's sinfulness.

Places of worship need the reviving presence of God. Solomon understood that it is possible to build a magnificent house of worship without much of God's presence. Solomon also knew he could never revive himself. His seeking after God shows he agreed with Charles Spurgeon, who wrote centuries later, "You would just as soon expect a wounded soldier on the battlefield to heal himself without medicine, or get himself to a hospital when his arms and legs have been shot off as you would expect to revive yourself without the help of God."[3]

After the Temple was completed, God answered Solomon's prayer, "If my people, who are called by my name, will humble themselves and pray and seek my face and turn from their wicked ways, then will I hear from heaven and will forgive their sin and will heal their land" (2 Chron. 7:14). A common theme keeps appearing: Although revival comes from God, we have an important role in bringing it to pass.

John gave God's formula for revival. A pattern for revival is clearly spelled out in the apostle John's warning to the Church at Ephesus. He begins by complimenting the noble achievements of the congregation. He commends them for good deeds, hard work, persevering tenacity, refusal to follow false apostles, and willingness to endure hardships. This list of admirable qualities is desirable for any church!

"Yet . . ."

"Yet, you have forsaken your first love." All their impressive achievements had little significance without a return to their first love. After issuing a solemn warning, John tells the Ephesian church members they will be renewed if they (1) remember the heights from which they have fallen; (2) repent; and (3) repeat the things they did at the beginning (see Rev. 2:1-6).

The warning, intended especially for the Ephesians, also applies to us: "He who has an ear, let him hear what the Spirit says to the churches" (Rev. 2:7). A first love lost is the problem, and rediscovering first love is the solution.

The ancient prophet has a demanding word too. A renewal passage in Hosea speaks to contemporary churches: "Sow for yourselves righteousness, reap the fruit of unfailing love, and break up your unplowed ground; for it is time to seek the LORD, until he comes and showers righteousness on you" (Hos. 10:12).

Many Churches Need a Heartwarming

Many churches are orthodox in doctrine and are busy in worthwhile activity but, like the Ephesians, have lost their first love. Some of these churches have pastors who know Scripture well and preach sermons decked out in impressive scholarship, generously seasoned with secular self-help suggestions. But something is missing, so neither pastors nor parishes glow with childlike faith, unpretentious obedience, and holy joy.

Because of lost love, outsiders regrettably find little warmth or nourishment in these fellowships. Years ago, Baptist evangelist Vance Havner described our current situation in words that sound like this morning's newspaper, "While we cry out against liberalism and loose living, are we not blind to the perils of lukewarmness? . . . Call it what you will, we need a heart-warming."[4]

Today, some churches toy, or even trifle, with revival. Like a small child with a short attention span on Christmas morning, many contemporary churches keep checking the ecclesiastical smorgasbord of the latest fads, looking for easier ways to do ministry. Magic quick-fix programs that cost little soul passion and require less commitment are sought.

Sometimes, an entire congregation tries to make itself believe that a religious performance is an actual revival or that an overly energetic worship service is genuine renewal. Performance, great crowds, and noise are not in themselves useful criteria. It is amazingly easy to fool ourselves into believing we are being renewed, when inside we are dried up.

Most of this is like fool's gold—a shoddy substitute for the real thing. Inside we are dying for a fresh infilling of God. Inside we are dry and barren and a long way from what God wants us to be.

Ministry Is a Dangerous Occupation

I recently talked with an insurance underwriter who ranks pastors among the safest actuarial risks a life insurance company can have from a physical point of view. Yet, ministry can be among the most dangerous of all occupations spiritually.

The cause of this risk, of course, is the enemy of our souls who ambushes ministers with sly snares and subtle temptations. An ineffective, compromised, or fallen pastor makes the devil's labors easier and more convincing. The enemy gets more credit than he deserves. Often our problems are self-induced by neglected prayer life, self-sufficiency, or professional pride.

The prophetic words written by Charles Spurgeon in the last century should cause us to stand at full spiritual attention: "We too often flog the church when the whip should be laid on our own shoulders. We should always remember that we are a part of the church, and that our own lack of revival is in some measure the cause of the lack of revival in the church at large. I will lay the charge before us; we ministers need a revival of piety in our lives. I have abundant grounds to prove it."[5]

REVIVALS START WITH HOLY DISSATISFACTION

Earlier in this chapter, we considered how God builds the need of revival and the hope for renewal into the fabric of Scripture. Scripture frequently warns us about the tendency of spiritual fire going out.

It reminds us, too, that organized religion nearly always continues its rituals and rules and regulations long after it has lost its soul. But in six words, John the apostle clinches the truth and stops all our defenses, "You have forsaken your first love."

Regardless of our theological label—evangelicals, liberals, conservatives, independents, charismatics, Catholics, reformed, Calvinists, Wesleyans—we all know John is right. The Church's first love has been forsaken. Incriminating evidence is everywhere. Every segment of Christianity has in some measure forsaken its first love and lost spiritual influence in society in the process.

How bad will it get before every pastor personally begins to stir up holy dissatisfaction with the way things are in his or her own soul and in the church?

Dissatisfaction 1: Loss of First Love

A long time ago, a ministry examination board asked a student pastor, "What does repentance mean?"

The young man replied, "To have a godly sorrow for sin."

The chairman of the examination board said, "You are only partly right. Repentance means to have a godly sorrow for sin, but it also means a willingness to forsake one's sins forever."

Sorrow and a willingness to forsake are important directives for the modern church. The Church in general, and local congregations in particular, have many reasons to repent. You can list your own convincing reasons. But even a very short list must include confused priorities, lukewarmness, shallowness, sin, diluted message, and inappropriate use of moneys contributed for ministry.

For too long, contemporary congregations have given themselves high marks because they worked hard, persevered, and refused to follow false prophets. But John clearly told the Ephesians that was good but not good enough for God. The church at Ephesus did those things well, and John still called them to repentance and insisted that they needed to return to their first love (see Rev. 2:1-6).

Dissatisfaction 2: Leaders with Sin in Their Lives

A church is never what God wants it to be when those who lead are living in sin. God's holy standards apply to laity and clergy equally. To the Corinthians, Paul wrote about sexual immorality in the church, "And you are proud! Shouldn't you rather have been filled with grief and have put out of your fellowship the man who did this?" (1 Cor. 5:2).

In God's expectations for His Church, willful sin disqualifies a person for leadership. The Father's serious concerns likely include sins we do not often worry about in church leaders, such as lying, cheating, doublespeak, gossip, stealing, and greed.

Biblical standards of the holy life must be applied to all who lead the Church in any way. Otherwise the Church becomes a sham and pretense and travesty in the eyes of her people and the community. Teachers, singers, decision makers, worship leaders, praise team members, all must live lives that are pleasing to God and inspiring to the congregation.

Pastors must rid their churches of sin. It must be done carefully, redemptively, and tenderly, but it must be done. Too often people, because their talent is so badly needed, are allowed to lead when they are spiritually unqualified. But yieldedness to Christ is the first key to Kingdom service and not talent alone.

Six facts must be faced in dealing with sin in leaders:
- God wants leaders to be holy.
- People in the pews know more about a leader's lifestyle than we think.
- Spiritually unqualified leaders often get right with God when a pastor urges change.
- If spiritual charades are allowed to continue, the offenders may eventually lose their souls.
- Spiritually unqualified leaders generally create an unwholesome drag on a church's ministry.
- Outsiders may never come to church because they know leaders are not living as they should.

Dissatisfaction 3: The Church Becomes Worldly-Minded

Worldliness chooses secular values rather than Kingdom priorities. Worldliness allows sophistication, security, and self-sovereignty to press us into secular ways of thinking and acting. Worldliness is playacting, leaving the impression of being holy, separate, and devoted when we are not.

For 2,000 years, the Church has crippled itself when it allowed the spirit and values of the world to shape its ministry. For some sad reason, each new generation has to learn this lesson. The secular world and a spiritual church do not mix any better than oil and water.

Worldliness sometimes shows in churches as a group pride of achievement or pride of spiritual commitment or pride of worship practices. Pride of achievement has been the downfall of churches who allow themselves to be distracted by their prominence, talent, or even their missionary efforts. In the process, some great old churches and some contemporary emerging congregations have become only an echo of what they could be in the kingdom of Christ.

Some congregations pride themselves in their piety. Being super-spiritual, these churches easily drift into becoming a holy club that admits only those who act and look a certain way—usually some weird way. They are separate for the sake of being separate but fail to realize that spiritual pride is actually sly, self-deceiving worldliness.

Worship practices also can become a subtle form of worldliness for churches. Some churches are proud of worn-out worship forms that no longer inspire anyone or that are little understood. Other churches are proud, believing they are special to God because of the energy, enthusiasm, or noise level of their services. Why the pride in either extreme?

Worship forms are nothing more than channels to help people into the presence of God; forms are never an end in themselves.

Worldliness can also infect a church's methods. In a day of shifting paradigms with many innovative ways of thinking and doing, many church leaders assume any method that is new or produces visible results is acceptable to God. A not-so-holy pragmatism sometimes makes us believe any means justifies the end, when the means and the end often need to be reevaluated in light of the New Testament. Although worldliness may not be in the method, it can be in the attitude of those who use the method.

Dissatisfaction 4: A Church Loses Its Sense of Wonder

Your church has amazing reasons to praise God. According to Peter, "But you are a chosen people, a royal priesthood, a holy nation, a people belonging to God, that you may declare the praises of him who called you out of darkness into his wonderful light" (1 Pet. 2:9).

That too-good-to-be-true news renews our sense of wonder. Think of it: The Father makes nobodies into a chosen people. If God says we really are a royal priesthood, a holy nation, a people belonging to God, we must be. That means every congregation has lots of reasons to praise God.

Peter says believers are no longer ordinary folks. God has made us different and alive and new, so we have incredible reasons to praise Him. Every church needs more praise to God for who He is helping them become.

Thousands of churches could be revolutionized in a week if they began to practice the motto, "Praise changes things." Or maybe the motto should be adjusted a bit, "Praise changes people who praise God." Rejoice in the wonders of God's grace that surround you in your congregation.

WHEN IS REVIVAL NEEDED?

Charles G. Finney offered a list to determine when a church needs a revival. The list from his revival lectures is timeless. He believed revivals were needed when these conditions prevailed.

- Lack of love: "When there is a lack of brotherly love and Christian confidence among professors of religion, then revival is needed."
- Disunity and division: "When there are dissensions and jealousies and evil speakings among professors of religion, then revival is needed."

- Worldliness: "When there is a worldly spirit in the church, then revival is needed."
- Sin in the church: "When the church finds its members falling into gross and scandalous sins, then revival is needed."
- Controversy and disagreement: "When there is a spirit of controversy in the church, then revival is needed."
- Wickedness controls society: "When the wicked triumph over the churches and revile them, then revival is needed."
- Sinners are careless: "When sinners are careless and stupid, then revival is needed."[6]

Genuine Revivals Start with Prayer

Seldom have great spiritual awakenings come to pastors, churches, or countries without intercessory prayer. John Hyde, a praying missionary, before an awakening in India near the turn of this century, asked Christians these questions to stimulate faithfulness in prayer for revival:

- Are you praying for quickening in your own life, in the life of your fellow workers, and in the church?
- Are you longing for greater power of the Holy Spirit in your life and work, and are you convinced you cannot go on without this power?
- Will you pray that you may not be ashamed of Jesus?
- Do you believe that prayer is the great means for securing this spiritual awakening?
- Will you set apart one-half hour each day as soon after noon as possible to pray for this awakening, and are you willing to pray till the awakening comes?[7]

REVIVAL REVOLUTIONIZES A CHURCH

Real revival restores an individual and a church to spiritual health and well-being. For an individual, genuine revival enables him or her to live out his or her faith in the daily details of life.

Such a renewal brings a church from subnormal, barely-making-it Christianity to a supernatural empowerment, a refreshing, a renewal, a sense of anointing, and a growing awareness that the Church is a unique organization owned and energized by God.

It stirs a congregation and challenges and empowers us to live out the radical demands of Christianity in every phase of life inside and outside the church.

Spiritual Normalcy Is Restored

The main purpose of renewal and revival is not to produce super-saints or souped-up churches, although that sometimes occurs. Revival more often directs a church to its original purposes, making it more wholesome, healthy, and robust or even redemptive. After restitution, forgiveness, and reordering of priorities are experienced by a church, re-newal and revival help believers sharpen their commitments to the church's unique roles and functions of prayer, worship, witness, and service. Spiritual normalcy then returns so that a church is more than a feeble imitation of a garden club, a service club, or a well-intentioned welfare organization.

Recently, a Southern California pastor shared a story of his person-al journey of faith. He told about joyous renewal in the congregation he serves and expressed the belief that pastoral renewal and congregational revitalization grow in the same spiritual soil. He believes renewal in one person encourages renewal in the other.

Revival made incredible changes in his church. Early prayer meet-ings following the Korean pattern of morning prayer replaced a clut-tered whirl of purposeless activities. His entire church is permeated with evidence of answered prayer. A new love for Scripture moves like wild-fire through the fellowship so people, wherever they gather, apply the meaning of the Bible to contemporary life. A changed, energetic wor-ship atmosphere is so common that parishioners often sing with mean-ing, "Surely the presence of the Lord is in this place." The pastor's ser-mons have a new passion and vitality.

No one can explain the amazing change because the church has the same preacher, the same songs, the same meeting time, the same worshipers, and the same sanctuary. Holy living has become the routine practice of many people in the church. The pastor suggested, "My peo-ple often say the Early Church must have been a lot like the present en-vironment in our church."

Extraordinary Prayer Is Activated

Evangelists and devotional writers are not agreed on whether prayer brings renewal or whether renewal engenders new power in prayer. It is like the chicken or the egg question. Either way, genuine re-vival always brings with it a component of extraordinary prayer.

It is a supernatural and satisfying kind of prayer in which the be-liever approaches God with a sense of humility and urgency—staying until he or she knows communication with God has occurred. Then he or she departs fully aware of having an audience with the King of the universe. It is the closest of all possible contacts with God.

Prayer is among the most popular discussion topics in church circles. We talk about prayer. We read books about prayer. We preach about prayer. We teach about prayer.

Meanwhile, it seems that the Church does not pray much. Now, the Church needs a bold urgency and fresh fervency in prayer until we know the answer is on the way because the Lord has heard us pray. It is still true, and God will continue to respond because, "The prayer of a righteous man is powerful and effective" (James 5:16). Magnificent answers to critical needs for renewal come when believers really pray.

Sin Feared as a Spiritual Cancer

Revival forces a person to face sin and its incredibly damaging consequences. Sin, like cancer, requires radical surgery if a person or church is to experience spiritual health. But worse than the dreaded effects of cancer on a human being is the not-so-obvious damage that individual sins have on a congregation. The outcome impacts a church, sometimes hindering its ministry for generations. Sin is serious business that must be acknowledged, forgiven, and forsaken.

Although it may not make us comfortable to think about it, many churches are crippled, anemic, handicapped, feeble, and too weak for spiritual warfare because of known and unknown, inner and outer, respectable and vile sin in their fellowship. Sometimes even in the ministry.

The remedies are the same as they have always been: intercessory prayer by everyone who cares about the spiritual well-being of the church, anointed preaching on the subject that is clearly based on Scripture, and an atmosphere of deliverance in the church where recent converts are encouraged to freely tell of their transformations from the sins of their past.

Miracles Are Experienced

Many debates among ministers and scholars center around the meaning of the term "signs and wonders." Some consider signs and wonders as flamboyant, absolutely unexplainable events, while others believe that the days of miracles ended with the apostles. Sincere Christ followers can be found on both sides of the issue.

Wherever you stand in the debate, it is time to admit that the contemporary Church needs more of the supernatural and miraculous. More ministers need to put themselves in places of courageous commitment that are so demanding and so near the cutting edge that it requires God's supernatural enablement to survive or thrive.

A veteran pastor remarked recently, "Don't expect a miracle until you have gone way beyond your own resources. God doesn't waste the supernatural on what you can do on your own."

Peter, the coward before Pentecost, did this in the Early Church. In Acts 4:29-30, Peter's (and the Church's) prayer for "signs and wonders" asks God for boldness to speak convincingly before Herod and Pontius Pilate and for supernatural results in the Early Church.

Peter received boldness and results. He wanted the Early Church to be so unique and so remarkable that no one could doubt it was an instrument of God. He prayed for results to impress those who watched the Church from the outside and to inspire those on the inside.

God answered Peter's prayer. The Bible says the place was shaken. They were filled with the Holy Spirit. They spoke the Word of God boldly. They were united. They shared everything they had, including their material possessions. They testified with great power of the Resurrection. They fed the needy. They sold their land for the cause of Christ, and all of them received much grace.

When you consider what the church would have been without this miraculous answer to prayer, Acts 4:32-35 is a model of God giving a church exactly what it needed, more than it expected, and more than members of the congregation thought they needed. It started when Peter prayed.

Results will be like that in our revivals. God will give us what we need. The work of God in the human heart and in the Church may not always be spectacular, but it will be supernatural.

National TV recently reported a story about a young Christian mother who refused to have a C-section performed because her unborn child was in medical trouble. She eventually delivered a healthy son naturally. Cynical media representatives did not know what to say, while many people accurately called it a miracle. We love the unusual and spectacular in the Church, but God also has many nonsensational miracles He wants to give every pastor and every church.

The Supernatural Continues Today

What about those close-at-hand and less sensational miracles that seldom are noticed? Here are a few that changed someone's world, but no one reported them to the press.

• Recently, a Bible college student's family in our town received

$100 in the mail from an unexpected source on the day their cupboards were empty.

- A few months ago, a rebellious teenager who had been living on the streets called her Christian parents and asked to come home after being led to Christ by a street preacher.

- A short while ago, a group of laypersons confronted a church controller and told him they were tired of him dominating the church, forcing pastors' resignations, and giving the church a bad name in the community. The controller left in a mad huff. Now in sweet fellowship, the lay leaders have concluded they will no longer be ruled by one person. The parting was a miracle that produced unity and peace.

- A few months ago, a minister who falsely accused a brother minister of stealing money from the church called to try to make things right. Although damages to the accused's reputation can never be fully restored, healing has started.

- Five years ago, a key layman in a middle-size church was gloriously called to the Christian ministry at age 35. His wife, unwilling to give up her home and security, openly opposed the idea. Wisely, the man simply said, "I won't make efforts to prepare until you agree wholeheartedly." He loved her, never badgered her, waiting for God's timing. God did a wonderful work in her heart and they are now students at a seminary.

Contemporary pastors need to pray Peter's prayer for their ministry setting. Who knows what God wants to do for you where you are. It might not be spectacular, but it could be supernatural.

What might happen if contemporary congregations received and used what God gave to the Church in Acts 4:32-35? Consider the remarkable possibilities for renewal in our time. They preached with supernatural power, they were filled with the Holy Spirit, they were committed to a common cause, they testified to the resurrection of Jesus, they had great grace, they gave up their security and greed by selling land, and they cared for the needy. Sounds like the supernatural power of God working in a local congregation, doesn't it?

Love Becomes Magnetic

When a revival of love occurs in a church, people treat each other as they would treat Christ. The golden rule becomes spontaneous. Differences are confessed, splintered relations are repaired, and restitutions are made.

Forgiveness is requested and granted. One person says, "I'm sorry" while another says, "It's OK; I should have grown past our disagreement months ago."

The glorious gift of hospitality gets dusted off. They baby-sit for each other. They became surrogate grandparents to children and love their young parents. They begin praying for each other and with each other. Love flows like a quiet river into every cranny of the church, so everyone sings better, smiles more, and criticizes less.

Like a holy epidemic, renewed love at church automatically spreads outside to offices, factories, gas stations, convenience stores, schools, Fortune 500 companies—wherever Christ lovers find themselves. Holy love flowing through the people of God to the unsaved is a powerful force for evangelism. Even though spiritually needy people may not be scolded out of their sins or reasoned into the Kingdom, they can often be loved to Jesus.

In this renewal of love, a believer's witnessing becomes delightful and natural. It shows on the tennis court, on the golf course, in shopping malls, in family rooms, in PTA meetings, and anywhere else we meet someone who needs the Savior. Outsiders who feel that love want to attend the church. And they often come again and again to experience the love of Christ flowing through a Christ-exalting church.

IT'S TIME TO LIGHT REVIVAL FIRES

While pleading for revival, Charles Spurgeon challenged laypeople to stop complaining about their pastors and to stop finding fault with their churches.

He challenged laity to cry out in intercessory prayer, "O Lord, revive Thy work in me!" He told laity, "You don't need a new preacher, another kind of worship, another type of preaching, new ways of doing things or even new people. You need life in what you have."[8]

Pastors need to hear a comparable message. This might be the time to get past the common and destructive "if only we had" syndrome. I've said it often and heard it many times in many places. Oh, if only we had another building. Oh, if only we had more trained laypersons. Oh, if only we had more money. Oh, if only we had a higher class of people. Oh, if only we had more commitment among the laity. Oh, if only we had a different style of worship. Oh, if only we had better or different music. Oh, if only my spouse were more involved. Oh, if only we had more Bible teachers. Oh, if only we had more social standing in the community. Oh, if only we had . . .

Spurgeon prescribes a cure for our "if only we had" debilitating virus. With a passionate heart burden he says, "If you want to move a train, you don't need a new engine, or even ten engines—you need to light a fire and get the steam up in the engine you now have."[9]

Spurgeon continues, "It is not a new person or a new plan, but the life of God in them that the church needs. Let us ask God for it! Perhaps He is ready to shake the world at its very foundations. Perhaps even now He is about to pour forth a mighty influence upon His people which shall make the church in this age as vital as it ever was in any age that has passed."[10]

Let's light the fire and get up steam in the engines we already have and let's pray, "O Lord, revive Thy work in me!"

A SPIRITUALLY RENEWED PASTOR

The following testimony must have been written by a renewed pastor—the kind the Church and the world need now. I regret the source is unknown to me.

A Christian leader saw it on the wall of a pastor's home in rural Africa. I have a copy from a radio preacher dated 1981, and a Bible college student found it in the notes of a pastor who has been with the Lord for several years. At any rate, it needs a wide reading and a wider replication in contemporary pastors. My appreciation and thanks to the unknown author.

I am a part of the "fellowship of the unashamed." I have Holy Spirit power. The dye has been cast. I've stepped over the line. The decision has been made. I am a disciple of His. I won't look back, let up, slow down, back away or be still. My past is redeemed, my present makes sense and my future is secure. I am finished and done with low living, sight walking, small planning, smooth knees, colorless dreams, tame visions, mundane talking, chincy giving and dwarfed goals!

I no longer need pre-eminence, prosperity, position, promotions, plaudits or popularity. I don't have to be right, first, tops, recognized, praised, regarded or rewarded. I now live by Presence, lean by faith, love by patience, lift by prayer and labor by power.

My face is set, my gait is fast, my goal is heaven, my road is narrow, my way is rough, my companions few, my Guide reliable, my mission clear. I cannot be bought, compromised, detoured, lured away, turned back, diluted or delayed. I will not flinch in the face of sacrifice, hesitate in the presence of adversity, negotiate at the table of the enemy, ponder at the pool of popularity or meander in the maze of mediocrity.

I won't give up, shut up, let up or burn up till I've preached up, prayed up, paid up, stored up and stayed up for the cause of Christ.

I am a disciple of Jesus. I must go till He comes, give till I drop and preach till everyone knows.

And when He comes to get His own, He'll have no problems recognizing me . . . my colors will be clear.

That makes it clear, doesn't it?

Notes

1. Bessie Porter Head, "O Breath of Life," *Sing to the Lord*, No. 305. Public domain.

2. Quoted in Bill Bright, ed., *The Greatest Lesson I've Ever Learned* (San Bernardino, Calif.: Here's Life Publishers, 1991), 177.

3. Quoted in Richard J. Foster and James Bryan Smith, eds., *Devotional Classics* (San Francisco: HarperSanFrancisco, 1993), 334.

4. *Day by Day* (Grand Rapids: Baker Book House, 1953), 16.

5. Foster and Smith, *Devotional Classics*, 332.

6. Charles G. Finney, *Revival Lectures* (Grand Rapids: Fleming H. Revell, 1979), 17-19.

7. Quoted from a letter to Focus on the Family, January 12, 1994.

8. Foster and Smith, *Devotional Classics*, 335.

9. Ibid.

10. Ibid.

Ron Blake has been a pastor in the Church of the Nazarene for 20 years. He was the director of Clergy Services at Nazarene Headquarters. He is presently the senior pastor at Detroit First Church of the Nazarene.

7

The Fellowship of Believers
Ron Blake

GOD HAS GIVEN US A BEAUTIFUL GIFT BY MAKING US PART OF THE fellowship of believers. We are told that because of our relationship with Christ we have fellowship with God and with others in the community of faith. But what does the word "fellowship" mean? One constraint on our understanding stems from designating in most of our churches a particular room as the "fellowship hall." By doing this we may seem to be limiting our fellowship to a room in the church. Properly understood, fellowship transcends such a narrow category and finds the breadth of its true meaning in the Scriptures.

Understanding fellowship begins with the biblical declaration of our fellowship with God. "We proclaim to you what we have seen and heard, so that you also may have fellowship with us. And our fellowship is with the Father and with his Son, Jesus Christ" (1 John 1:3). The foundational understanding is that we have fellowship with the Father, His Son, and the Holy Spirit (albeit not explicitly stated here). It would be impossible to have fellowship with another believer if we were not in fellowship with the Father. "Fellowship" means "having in common"; this is what unites us, our relationship with the Father through Jesus Christ His Son. Thus we have something in common with fellow believers, namely, our relationship with Christ and thereby with the Father. Fellowship also communicates a companionship that comes from having things in common. Let us look at a few other scriptures to see how this companionship—this fellowship—should work itself out in the church.

In verse 7 of this same chapter we find this statement: "But if we walk in the light, as he is in the light, we have fellowship with one another, and the blood of Jesus, his Son, purifies us from all sin." Here we find that preserving our relationship with the Father—"walking in the light"—also preserves our fellowship with other believers. This is how we maintain community. Problems that threaten to divide our fellowship more easily find their resolution when all involved seek to maintain their companionship with a God who values self-sacrifice over self-promotion. In this passage clearly the continuance of our companionship with God is intertwined with that of our companionship with others. This also works in the reverse, as Matt. 5:23-24 advises regarding the restoration of good community relations before leaving a "gift . . . in front of the altar."

Another aspect of Christian community or fellowship is found in the Book of James: "Therefore confess your sins to each other and pray for each other so that you may be healed. The prayer of a righteous man is powerful and effective" (James 5:16). It seems foreign to our ears, this verse enjoining us to confess our sins to each other. Most of us have grown up in the Western world with our love of the "rugged individualist." We have a hard time understanding that while our faith is personal, it is never private. We are placed in a family of faith; we are a part of a team and must take into consideration the needs and feelings of others and be accountable to each other.

How much of what plagues us in life is a direct result of selfishness and self-centeredness? Many marriages suffer because one or both spouses are focused on themselves. It never seems to enter their minds to consider their spouses' needs—"How can I serve my spouse?" Yet constantly if you listen to folks coming for marital counseling, they are nearly always concerned that their spouses have not been meeting their needs. Evidently when they heard the pastor at their wedding ceremony say the "two shall become one," they thought they were the one. Again, it may be our culture's individualism that keeps us from healthy marital relationships.

Unfortunately, this can carry over into our way of relating in the church. If our congregations are filled with people who think this way, it may be hard to convince them that in the family of God we look out not just for our own interests but for the interests of others as well. Our culture has a sort of love affair with the myth of the lone person who stands against the crowd and wins the day. Many of us grew up with the proud example of the Lone Ranger—the fictional masked hero of the Old West who was accompanied by Tonto, his quiet sidekick, who seemed content merely to confirm the rightness of whatever the Lone Ranger did. The Lone Ranger did not consult with anyone but did everything his way, leaving people whom he had rescued to wonder as he rode off into the sunset, "Who was that masked man?" Many Christians conduct themselves as if they are 21st-century Lone Rangers. They ride off chasing after whatever thrill or program they believe will lead them to spiritual success, while only giving passing acknowledgment to the Body of Christ; they believe they are the best judges of what they need. Consulting, praying, learning, or growing together with other believers is unnecessary.

We may think we can get along fine by ourselves. But when we come to a verse like James 5:16 that tells us to confess our sins one to the other, we wonder how we can accomplish this in our world of independence and self-reliance? Is James saying there is more to Christian fellowship than sharing Styrofoam cups of coffee and doughnuts in Sunday School? Does he mean we might be able to help someone on this journey of faith? And even more radical, does he mean that someone might be able to help us? How much unnecessary suffering has taken place because we have isolated ourselves from community? How many poor decisions have been made because we failed to take into account the wisdom of other believers? Because we have not opened ourselves to the advice of others, we have not given counsel and advice to them. The cycle of not bearing one another's burdens is ongoing.

A major part of the problem is thinking that attending the Sunday morning worship service is the same as being in community and having fellowship with one another. While the worship service is certainly a component of fellowship and community, it is not the whole or entire system. Fellowship by its very nature involves knowing and being known. As in all other meaningful relationships, this kind of knowledge must be developed and nurtured over time—more time than just an hour or two each Sunday morning.

So what is this verse from James that seems so foreign to our understanding really saying to us? Namely, if we are a family and a fellowship, we are obligated to help each other in meaningful ways. Since sin is never really private, in spite of what our culture says, we need to help the community of faith deal with it properly. The natural reaction to sin is to hide it; this is done through denial, excuse making, and other methods of cover-up. Yet James says that we are to confess our sins to each other. This verse seems to be a biblical antidote to the isolated, individualistic Christianity so prevalent in our world. Sin touches more than the one involved; thus it must be corrected with the help of the community. We need to be accountable to both Christ and His church.

Folks might be resistant to this understanding because many in the church are more interested in gossip than in restoring a fallen brother or sister. We cannot expect people to confess their sins to each other if they know someone is going to make them headliners on the prayer chain. Nurturing the importance of keeping confidences and being trustworthy will go far in encouraging the openness needed for accountability to flourish.

This verse also mentions that we should "pray for each other." One of the great strengths of having fellowship is the ability to pray for and with each other. There is power in praying for each other. This passage also indicates that there is healing available through such mutual prayer.

To accountability and prayer, Heb. 10:24-25 adds another nuance to our understanding of fellowship: "And let us consider how we may spur one another on toward love and good deeds. Let us not give up meeting together, as some are in the habit of doing, but let us encourage one another—and all the more as you see the Day approaching." A part of our fellowship ministry is that of spurring each other on. Encouragement is a major component of the fellowship of believers. It is quite easy to become discouraged, and with that comes feelings of negativity and self-pity. A part of this mutual encouragement is the need to remind each other that love is always the way. Love is the glue that holds us together. It is the adhesive contact in our fellowship together. "By this all men will know that you are my disciples, if you love one another" (John 13:35).

Jesus was clear that love would be the identifying mark of discipleship. Interestingly, He did not say that this would be the mark to help believers identify other believers but that this would be the way the world would identify believers. We will not win the world by our clever arguments, impressive buildings, and first-class programs. We will not win it by how evangelistic and compassionate we are. What will win the world is our love for one another—our unconditional love. People in the world are looking for love—not looking for love alone—but looking for someone to love them unconditionally.

If we are serious about reaching the world for Christ, we must be equally serious about loving our brothers and sisters in Christ. This puts an entirely different face on our fellowship. We are not just to be nice to each other because that is the respectable thing to do; rather our Christlike fellowship should draw the world like a magnet. Perhaps it is entirely too optimistic, but one suggestion for us as congregations would be that rather than thinking up a new program to launch this fall, we instead decide to be a loving fellowship. We would not only strengthen our fellowship but also add to it an evangelistic characteristic. There is something so powerful about Christlike love that it draws people and causes them to wish for such fellowship for themselves. We should ask ourselves, "How can I be a more loving member of the fellowship? Who is it that I need to encourage in their walk with the Lord? How can I intentionally show a genuine Christian kind of love and encouragement?"

The passage in Hebrews also reminds us of another important component of Christian fellowship—that we are not to neglect gathering together for worship. This again emphasizes that the journey we are on is personal but not private. There are many things to be gained by worshiping together, but right at the top of the list is, as we've discussed, encouragement.

Something special happens when believers worship together: "For where two or three come together in my name, there am I with them" (Matt. 18:20). These oft-quoted words of Jesus say much to us regarding Christian fellowship. Yes, Christ is with me when I am at home, when I am traveling, and when I have my devotional time. But Jesus is reminding us that whenever a group of believers is together, He is there in the midst of them in a unique way. I have experienced wonderful times with the Lord in various places and at various times in my life, but I experienced His blessings in very special ways during those times I worshiped Him with other believers. Some of the most powerful times in my own life have been when God has ministered to me through the singing of believers, the testimony of a saint, the partaking of Communion, and the preaching of the Word. The fellowship of believers is important because when we gather together, Christ comes to us in a way that is powerfully and utterly different from how He meets us otherwise.

I believe we must make more people in the church aware of how important Christian fellowship is. Having been a pastor for 20 years, these last 3 years found me ministering in another capacity, and for the first time in my adult life I was a member and not the pastor of a local church. During this time I learned some valuable lessons. I learned that pastors (myself included) are truly unaware of the fellowship challenges facing our churches. Because people seek us out and want to talk to us, we assume that everyone in the congregation is similarly treated. But I found that no matter how intentional you are, it can still be very difficult to work your way into fellowship with other believers. Perhaps we pastors are so occupied with planning and executing worship services and plugging in new and better programs that we have forgotten that there are needs in the human experience that can only be helped with genuine and authentic Christian fellowship.

As a pastor I thought that if we planned enough activities after church on Sunday evening, we were doing fellowship correctly. After a three-year stint of not being a senior pastor, I found that holding a cup of coffee in the fellowship hall and grunting at church folks as they walked by me was not really fellowship but rather nothing more than drinking coffee by myself in a crowd. Whether we use the title small groups or Sunday School, we must intentionally bring people into a context where they can experience the deep relationships that constitute Christian fellowship.

While in my new assignment, I found myself in the hospital with an infection. Two pastors visited me; they prayed, quoted Scripture, and greatly encouraged me. Later on a man from the church I was attending showed up at my hospital door. He came in, and we engaged in small talk. He gave me a gift—a small book written by a famous Christian author. To this day I will never forget that he took the time to sit down and talk with me, expressing great compassion and interest. We each took turns sharing our hopes and even our fears, and he prayed for me in a simple yet powerful way. As I am writing these words, I am still gripped with the emotion that floods over me from my memories of that evening. After he left the room, I knew I had just experienced fellowship; we did not have a cup of coffee, yet we had shared as Christian brothers. I am not sure that I encouraged him, but he definitely encouraged me.

For genuine fellowship to take place believers must commit both their time and themselves. This gentleman had worked all day, left his wife at home, and drove across the city to spend a significant amount of time with me. I know we generally refer to this as congregational care or outreach, but most significantly this kind of sharing together and encouraging of each other fits the biblical definition of Christian fellowship. When true fellowship occurs, we are left no doubt about its identity; it leaves with us the joyful traces of having loved and been loved by one of God's own.

George G. Hunter III, Ph.D., was a fish out of water the summer of '62. As a young seminary student, he spent eight weeks sharing his faith with "Muscle Beach" surfers, beatniks, and body builders. They thought he was from another planet; church jargon made little sense to them. That experience sent Hunter on a lifetime quest that has placed him among the world's leading authorities on communicating the gospel to secular people. A coveted speaker, Dr. Hunter has led seminars for more than 30 denominations in more than 20 different countries. He has authored 10 books, including *To Spread the Power: Church Growth in the Wesleyan Spirit* (1987), *How to Reach Secular People* (1992), *Church for the Unchurched* (1996), *The Celtic Way of Evangelism* (2000), *Leading and Managing a Growing Church* (2000), and *Radical Outreach* (2003)—all with Abingdon Press.

Dr. Hunter has served the United Methodist Church in a variety of ways, ranging from pastor to executive for the Board of Discipleship's section on Evangelism, a role in which he oversaw the evangelistic program for the denomination's 38,000 churches. He is the cofounder of the American Society for Church Growth and founder of the Academy for Evangelism in Theological Education. He is married to the former Ella Fay Price and has three children: Gill, Monica, and Donald. "Muscle Beach" impacted Hunter in more ways than one. He still lifts weights "religiously," and competed in three bench-press contests after turning 50. After claiming first place in one, his kids labeled him "Elvis Press."

Hunter came to Asbury in 1983 to serve as founding dean of the E. Stanley Jones School of World Mission and Evangelism; he served as dean for 18 years. In 2001, Hunter was named Asbury Seminary's first distinguished professor.

8

Examining the "Natural Church Development" Project

George G. Hunter III

🍃 MORE THAN A FEW AMERICAN CHURCH LEADERS ARE ENGAGED, enamored, even captivated by a "new" approach to church growth—as attractively featured in Christian Schwarz's *Natural Church Development* (translated and published in English by ChurchSmart Resources, 1996). Schwarz, a German church leader, led a team of people who surveyed some 1,000 churches, in 18 languages, in 32 countries, over a 10-year period. The team believes that church growth necessarily follows from "church health"—as defined by the team's "eight essential qualities of healthy churches." When churches focus on attaining the known qualities of healthy churches, *Natural Church Development* says churches should experience those very qualities in greater measure and should grow as a result. Stressing the importance of the adjectives, these are the qualities featured:

1. Empowering Leadership
2. Gift-Oriented Ministry
3. Passionate Spirituality
4. Functional Structures
5. Inspiring Worship
6. Holistic Small Groups
7. Need-Oriented Evangelism
8. Loving Relationships

The Natural Church Development (NCD) organization works with churches that want greater health and growth. The NCD web site <www.ncd-international.org> reports that the organization has worked with 22,000 churches on six continents and claims that 85 percent experienced subsequent growth. (The web site does not report, however, what percent of the churches were already growing or what percent increased their growth rate to a statistically significant degree or for how long.)

The "diffusion" of NCD's model has been remarkably uneven. Many pastors and other local church leaders swear by it; busy people have often found church growth writings "too complicated," so they understandably gravitate toward a resource with the appearance of a manual or even a recipe. Likewise, some judicatory or denominational executives have put all their eggs in the NCD basket. NCD, however, registers no blip at all on many other radar screens. Schwarz's book has never been reviewed in the *Journal for the Scientific Study of Religion* or the *Review of Religious Research*. The leading sociologist of religion, Rodney Stark, tells me that he has never heard of Schwarz or his book. Lyle Schaller, who knows more about churches than anyone else who ever lived, read *Natural Church Development* but saw it as methodologically flawed—because its conclusions depend entirely upon the subjective self-reporting of church members. A divided response to NCD can inhabit a single institution; the doctor of ministry people at both Fuller and Asbury are much more attracted to NCD than are the school of mission people at the same institutions.

Most of the leaders of the American Society for Church Growth, who want the church health and growth that NCD wants, regard the project as promising more than it delivers, as claiming more than it achieves, and as methodologically flawed and conceptually dubious. Two empiricists, John Ellas and Flavil Yeakley, published in the society's journal the only thorough analysis of NCD that I have found.[1] That review and discussions of NCD in the society's meetings and other settings have focused on these kinds of observations:

1. Regarding NCD's claim to originality: Some of the NCD team's work represents some original or fairly original pioneering.

 a. The study attempts a "scientific," statistical, quantitative, comprehensive study of church growth, though it is *not* the first quantitative church growth study.

 b. In a departure from the stream of church growth studies since the 1970s, NCD focuses on church "health" more than most, though it was not the first, and NCD's allegation that most church growth writers are uninterested in congregational health would be impossible to demonstrate. "Internal" (or "quality") church growth has always been prominent in church growth lore.

    c. NCD's claim that a church experiences new health and growth by focusing on its weaknesses among the eight characteristics of health is fairly original; most scholars in organization leadership have advised organizations to identify and build upon their strengths. (The truth is no doubt located somewhere in between. For instance, if a church's greatest comparative weakness is evangelism, the church would likely grow through more and better evangelism; but transition into a more "functional structure" might not, by itself, bring greater growth.)

    d. Some NCD claims to *original* insight are not warranted. The chapter on "functional structures," for instance, claims, "Our research confirmed for the first time an extremely negative relationship between traditionalism and both growth and quality within the church." If, prior to Schwarz, this connection was a secret, it was a badly kept secret. Many scholars have observed this connection. There was no one in the church growth field who did not already know that!

    e. In a remarkable apparent contradiction, NCD claims that traditionalism may be OK in worship! "Services may target Christians or non-Christians, their style may be liturgical or free, their language may be 'churchy' or secular—it makes no difference for church growth." The fact is that for most "pre-Christian" populations, in most places, services welcoming seekers that begin where the seekers are and employ language (and other cultural forms) they understand engage more pre-Christian people and make more new disciples.

2. Regarding the NCD research methodology:

    a. The study gathered from 30 people in 1,000 churches the self-perceptions of those members about their churches and then assumed that self-reported self-perceptions are facts. Three (not so hypothetical) cases can easily undermine this assumption: A church's "builder generation" people may experience an organ interlude from Bach's Mass in B Minor as "inspiring worship"; but young pre-Christian visitors, raised more on rock than Bach, might not. Again, church members often report "loving relationships" within their fellowship only to be astonished that, say, the pre-Christian young woman with an addiction and a reputation does *not* experience the fellowship the same way. Again, John Ellas distributed the NCD survey instrument in the congregation he attends. He reports: "Members' perceptions of congregational strengths were highly inaccurate in numerous categories." For instance, members rated their church's "need-oriented evangelism" fourth highest among the eight characteristics; Ellas reports, however, that the church had no notable evangelism emphasis in the preceding five years, and it experienced less than half the conversion growth rate we typically observe in growing churches.[2]

b. Schwarz's *Natural Church Development* does not provide enough data or detail for other researchers to replicate the study, nor even enough to understand the basis of the conclusions.

c. Schwarz does not report the significance level of his conclusions; without the significance level, empiricists tell us, no statistical study should be relied upon.

d. The study claims to present the universal causes of church health and growth, but it only presents *correlations*—which are alleged but not sufficiently demonstrated. Empiricists would caution us, however, that (some or all) of the eight qualities *might* produce church health and growth. However, church growth may produce the climate in which members have positive perceptions of (some or all of) these qualities. Again, both the health and the growth may be caused by other variables, as I will suggest below.

e. NCD passes off, as original, many insights that are patently *not* original, and without citing the earlier sources whose insights they repeat. (In some quarters, that is called plagiarism; it is not permitted in any respectable graduate program.) As one of many examples, Win Arn demonstrated in the 1980s, from surveys in hundreds of churches, the correlation between the people's perceptions of love (toward each other in the church and toward the outside community) and the growth of the church.[3]

f. Ellas and Yeakley reported that after 7 years of NCD's 10-year study, a consultant identified several serious flaws in their instrument and their testing procedure. To NCD's credit, they fixed the instrument and the procedure; to their discredit, they based their conclusions on the data from the whole 10 years![4]

    g. Most church growth researchers would say that NCD methodology comes up shortest at two points. First, they failed to give priority to the gathering of data from new converts; every serious church growth researcher knows that new converts are, after all, the population pool most capable of telling how and why they found faith and joined the church; the pastor and established members often do *not* know why their church is reaching pre-Christian people. Second, NCD relied too much on number crunching from questionnaires that people filled out; only interviews can confirm the people's understanding of the questions, probe deeply enough to access their experiences, and engage their knowledge they may not yet have verbalized, and only interviews (with skilled field observation) can identify many of the real causes of church health and growth.

3. Regarding NCD's conclusions:

    a. Most church growth people do not know what to do with NCD's conclusions, because NCD does not distinguish between the most fundamental ways in which a local church grows—biological growth, transfer growth, and conversion growth. That semantic blur may help account for one of NCD's claims, that "services may target Christians or non-Christians, their style may be liturgical or free, their language may be 'churchy' or secular—it makes no difference for church growth." It may make no difference in transfer growth; indeed, many mobile Christians prefer to join another liturgically traditional church. It does make a significant difference virtually everywhere in a church's outreach to pre-Christian populations. It is almost impossible to find churches experiencing significant conversion growth from the world through, say, traditional music. The only exceptions do *not* do the old music "the same old way"; they invest the music with greater complexity, energy, and improvisation; they follow a revised composition; they accompany it with contemporary instrumentation; and the old music is thereby experienced as contemporary. (Listen to the Brooklyn Tabernacle Choir's rendition of the "Hallelujah Chorus" from Handel's *Messiah*, for example.)

    b. The chapter on "loving relationships" in *Natural Church Development* displays a lack of knowledge regarding the meaning of *agape* love in the New Testament. While NCD reports that they used a dozen variables in assessing the love in churches, the only two they feature—laughter in the church and spending time together outside the church—do not necessarily indicate the presence of *agape* love, especially love for lost people. Christian love is, undoubtedly, an essential feature of healthy growing churches, but NCD does not appear to have demonstrated it and may not understand it.

c. NCD's people do their project a disservice by the artificial device of attaching only one adjective to each of the characteristics. Truth is never that simple, and what is going on is never that singular. For instance, most leadership studies indicate that it is as important for leaders to be "visionary" as it is to be "empowering," and being "obedient" is arguably more important in spirituality than being "passionate." Again, devotees of the Saddleback SHAPE acronym (Spiritual Gifts, Heart, Abilities, Personality type, and Experiences) are convinced that discovering one's spiritual giftedness is less empowering for ministry than a more complete understanding of how the Holy Spirit has "shaped" us for ministry.

d. In some cases, the favored adjective overstates what NCD has demonstrated. For instance, NCD reports a greater correlation between "small groups" and church growth than for any of the other seven characteristics, *but* they say the groups must be "holistic." Curiously, NCD says small groups are "holistic" *if* they study the Bible *and* apply it to their lives (regardless, apparently, of whether they pray or minister to each other or have any ministry or cause outside the group or welcome seekers into the group).

e. So NCD is wrong in emphasizing any one adjective more than the noun it modifies. It would be more strategic to emphasize the nouns and to nuance each noun with the one to several adjectives that do fuller justice to the research and to the characteristic than one adjective alone can do.

4. NCD's great omissions: NCD assumes, without sufficient warrant, that their eight characteristics are *the* eight characteristics of healthy, growing churches. It is possible, however, to identify other characteristics that are *at least* as normative for church health and growth as the eight that NCD emphasizes. I will feature eight more characteristics that are at least as essential to health and growth as most of the NCD's eight:

a. In the long history of the serious study of Christian mission, the greatest consensus is around the importance of *context;* to reach a people and grow among them, the Christian movement *must* adapt to their "macro-context." The faith spreads differently in desert communities than arctic communities, among nonliterate peoples than among formally educated peoples, among refugee populations than among suburbanites, among peoples with a vivid sense of the supernatural than peoples deeply influenced by the Enlightenment's "closed system" model of the cosmos. Mission scholars know that to ignore contexts and assume we can "do church" the same way everywhere is folly. Indeed, the definitive studies of effective organizations, of all kinds—from fast-food restaurants to automobile manufacturers to computer software companies to universities—substantially attribute their effectiveness to their understanding of, and strategic adaptation to, their general context, and to that context's ongoing changes. The NCD project seems to be oblivious to the supreme importance of understanding the "soils" in which we seek to plant the gospel seed.

b. NCD also seems to be oblivious, likewise, to the most important part of any church's context—the *culture* of the target population. We are certain, from a long history of mission studies, that ministry must be done in "indigenous" forms to engage most of the pre-Christian people of any society, in any and every field of mission. An indigenous strategy requires paying the price to understand the target culture, that is, the characteristic language, aesthetics, values, attitudes, beliefs, customs, style preferences, and (especially) the worldview themes of the people's consciousness. The assumption that churches can reach many people without understanding them and adapting to them culturally is a delusion.

c. The *credibility* of the church's people with a pre-Christian population is, undoubtedly, as important as any characteristic that NCD features. Helmut Thielicke observed in the secular West Germany of a generation ago that the single most important variable in whether or not the people will believe Christianity's message is the perceived credibility of the witnessing community. The academic study of communication has known, for 23 centuries, that the perceived credibility of an advocate powerfully affects a message's reception. My own field research with secular people, beginning in 1962, persistently indicates that in great numbers they want to know (a) whether we really believe it, (b) and/or whether we live by it, (c) and/or whether it makes enough difference to take seriously.

d. You would never know for sure from NCD whether growing churches are *in ministry* to people outside the church who are not yet disciples. You could infer this from the characteristic they name "need-oriented evangelism," but the term obscures as much as it reveals. To be more precise, more and more of the earth's contagious churches are reaching pre-Christian people through outreach ministries—from GED tutoring to literacy classes to a range of support groups, recovery ministries, and a hundred others. These outreach ministries are, indeed, need-oriented, and need-oriented witness is an indispensable part of outreach ministry but not the whole of it.

e. The NCD model seems to assume that a church can be quite "healthy" without a *social ethic*. But how "healthy" can a church be if it has no priority concern for justice, peace, reconciliation between peoples, or the health of the planet? I am astonished that some Christian scholars from Germany appear to have gained no enduring insight from the Third Reich, the Holocaust, World War II, and so on. Some of the German churches that slept through the 1930s, who expressed no prophetic challenge to evil, would have scored high on NCD's eight criteria!

f. The NCD model seems to assume that a church can be quite "healthy" without a wider *mission*. But how "healthy" can a church be without a deep involvement in Christ's wider mission, locally and globally?

g. The NCD model, undoubtedly in the attempt to provide a generic model useful to churches of all denominational traditions, ignores the fact that *strength in one's tradition* is also a sign of health. One example should suffice: How "healthy" is a Quaker church that is not engaged in peacemaking?

h. *Always* there are *local contextual factors* that need to be included in any normative faithful profile of a healthy church. If, say, the church's immediate ministry area has been "swamped" by a flood or hurricane, crime, job losses, a shooting at the high school, 80,000 Haitian immigrants, or vast numbers of secular people with no Christian memory, each local church needs the latitude to shape its ideal health model according to the challenges presented by the immediate context. Local contexts vary so enormously that a recipe or manual that, like the proverbial stretch sock, will fit every situation is impossible to produce, and the quest for it is delusional. Churches succeed locally or not at all.

I should approach a conclusion by putting the current wide interest in church health in historical perspective. Some church leaders now assert that church growth is dated, that church health has taken its place and is now *in*. However, since church growth serves as shorthand for referring to the spread, expansion, or diffusion of Christianity, *and* for the field-research approach to informing effective evangelism, mission strategy, and the gospel's spread, the narrower focus on health could hardly take church growth's place.

Indeed, the current obsession with church health is little more than the church renewal of the 1960s and 1970s warmed over, with some differences. The church renewal people were more theologically grounded; the church health people are more interested in what churches are doing.

The present interest in church health, however, repeats the three big mistakes of the past: (1) It (mis)perceives evangelization as only one of eight or so priorities of the congregation; actually, evangelization is the apostolic congregation's main business. (2) Furthermore, it perpetuates the assumption that if a local church can only get renewed enough (or healthy enough), *then* it can, and will, reach out effectively; actually, churches that adopt the renewal-first model never get around to much outreach, because they never feel renewed (or healthy) enough. (3) Neither the church renewal people nor the church health people have discovered what is obvious to most church growth researchers: churches are renewed (or made healthier) more from a steady stream of new disciples entering the ranks than from all the known renewal ministries combined.

We should conclude by affirming much that we read in *Natural Church Development*. NCD's leaders want churches to experience greater health and growth, and they launched an ambitious project to give health and growth a clearer rationale and better footing. Some of their conclusions are undoubtedly valid, though because of problems with research instrument, design, and interpretation we cannot say which! Many church leaders are undoubtedly attracted to NCD's eight characteristics—largely, I suggest, because the themes, such as inspiring worship and loving relationships, confirm what they have intuitively believed all along!

Some churches are undoubtedly helped by NCD's model—in part, I surmise, because they believe in it enough to plan and act upon it. NCD acts, at least, like the proverbial "placebo" in medical studies—in which, say, the blood pressure improves almost as much in the experimental control subjects who took the placebo as those who took the experimental drug.

So we are grateful to NCD for the churches that believe in it enough to get a better act together. We are grateful to NCD for whatever they now hypothesize that ultimately turns out to be true. We are grateful to NCD for the visibility they have given, in some quarters, to issues of church health and church growth. We are grateful to NCD for provoking some of us in the church growth school of thought into a new period of field research, reflection, and clarification, and for the reminder to make church growth lore as simple as possible.

Notes

1. See John Ellas and Flavil Yeakley, review of *Natural Church Development*, by Christian A. Schwarz, *Journal of the American Society for Church Growth* 10 (spring 1999), 83-91.

2. Ibid., 90-91.

3. Win Arn, Carroll Nyquist, and Charles Arn, *Who Cares About Love?* (Monrovia, Calif.: Church Growth Press, 1986).

4. Ellas and Yeakley, 86-87.

Mary Rearick Paul copastors the St. Paul's Church of the Nazarene in Duxbury, Massachusetts, with her husband, Bruce. They have two sons—Wesley, age 13, and Jonathan (JJ), age 10. She graduated from Eastern Nazarene College with a degree in social work and Boston University with a master of divinity, and she has recently completed the course work necessary for a doctorate of ministry at Asbury Seminary. She was a participant in the Beeson Pastor Fellowship at Asbury Seminary. She has previously served as senior pastor at two Nazarene Churches: the First Church of the Nazarene in Lynn, Massachusetts, and the Bethel Church of the Nazarene in Quincy, Massachusetts.

9

Servant Evangelism

Mary Rearick Paul

❧ TWO WORDS ARE OFTEN TALKED ABOUT WITHIN THE CONFINES OF the church but are often lacking in significant ways in the life of the church. These words carry weight, for they are filled with the guilt of the ought-tos. These words are "servanthood" and "evangelism." As Christians, we understand that we are called to be servants, but life has a way of consuming all our extra energies before we ever get around to thinking of others. We also know that evangelism is supposed to be part of each of our lives, but most of us are either very uncomfortable at attempting to be evangelists or have been frustrated by our feeble, nonproductive efforts. We commit ourselves to both these activities with sporadic endeavors that quickly die out until guilt pushes us to try once again.

I remember my church sending me out as a teen with others my age to distribute brochures to our neighbors. We were quickly trained in some conversation starters that were to be followed up with a presentation of the gospel. I spent the day with my heart beating out of my chest as I quietly walked up front paths and tapped on doors, praying that no one would be home and thanking God when no one came to the door.

Service projects were easier to participate in, and I enjoyed those times when they occurred, but service geared to those outside the church walls seemed to be a yearly event rather than a regular life commitment. Nowadays churches usually remember to do some service projects around Thanksgiving and Christmas. But the focus is often on caring for "our own" first, such as the homebound elderly, fringe families, or extended relatives of members.

While these people are important to include in our ongoing care, the reality is we rarely move beyond them. Churches often become absorbed in a mission to care for "the family." This is far too narrow a scope when compared to the broad call to reach all people. This limitation of purpose ultimately marks the local church as more of a social club than a people with a mission.

The potential to offer the gospel's life-changing experience is significantly limited when a church decides to focus on caring for those inside the church walls. Tom Nees says, "If the mission of a congregation is to serve its member families wherever they live rather than serve the neighborhood that surrounds the church building, then when its families move, the church as a body of believers has in fact already moved—regardless of the building's location."[1] In fact the church's presence in a neighborhood becomes insignificant to the people who live in its vicinity.

Every Christian has to grapple with his or her own willingness to take on the nature of a servant. Thus every Christian's challenge is also to find ways to step out of the safe confines of the church walls and family groupings and offer the gospel to "all the world." There are many reasons why an adequate response to servanthood and evangelism is necessary for the Christian. There are scriptural mandates that inform and confirm this. There are benefits for the individual in meaning and significance as the person discovers the joy of entering a full ministry of reconciliation. Also, the local church can come to know a revitalized life as it engages in acts of love and grace. At the simplest level, God desires that we know His life in all its abundance. To know the joy and the meaning God desires to give us and give through us, we must find ways to engage in being people of service and evangelism. It is thus imperative that as pastors we find ways to be people in wholehearted response to these calls.

The call to serve has been the struggle of the ages. Humility is at the root of servanthood. The notion of a God who would choose the way of the Cross to communicate and transform continues to challenge His followers. Like the Israelites, we the church would often prefer a king who comes with subjecting power to put all things in order. Instead God comes and turns everything inside out through the power of transformative servanthood. God calls His followers to relate to the world in a similar way.

The theme of servanthood is presented throughout the Scriptures. A few examples would be the four servant songs found in Isaiah, Jesus' redefining greatness in Matt. 20:27-28 and 23:11, and the passage describing Jesus washing the feet of the disciples found in John 13:3-17. The Scriptures describe various leaders as servants. Moses is described in terms of humility and service. The references to Moses by God in the Scriptures designate him as "My servant Moses" (Num. 12:6-8, NASB) and as "very humble, more than any man who was on the face of the earth" (12:3, NASB). Joshua in turn is referred to as "the servant of the

LORD" (Josh. 24:29, NASB). Paul also designated himself a servant (Rom. 1:1; Phil. 1:1), and he proclaimed a theology of service. Phil. 2:1-11 (the "Christ Hymn") is one example of this servant emphasis.

Jesus is our primary Model of servanthood. He patterned an ongoing commitment to love all—friend and foe. His willingness to make sacrifices throughout His life all the way to death on the Cross was unprecedented. He caused great distress among the religious leaders as He included the excluded in His community. His willingness to engage a wide variety of people in conversation and to eat with them scandalized the religious folk of His day. He broke out of the confines of the religious community and called His disciples to do likewise.

When Jesus entered the world as a Suffering Servant, He did not come as a victim of the powers of the world but as a new kind of revealed power that transforms through serving the world. A service of humility that has the power to transform has implications for Christ's followers as they seek to live out the call of the Incarnation. The humility of Christ was revealed when He chose to dwell among the people, become vulnerable, and eat with the sinners. His servanthood was made evident when He loved people before their behavior had changed, such as in Mark 10 when He is portrayed as looking on the rich man with love even when the rich man's choice was not to follow Him. He loved those who betrayed Him. He cried, He laughed, He challenged, He listened, and He was patient with those who did not get His message or understand who He was. He, who was fully God, never considered any person beneath His attention, touch, or love. In fact He saved His harshest language for those religious folks who considered themselves better than others. It was an attitude of elitism and judgment that He could not abide. He who was God was willing to be born among us as a baby and grow up physically with all the developmental awkwardness that entailed.

God incarnate humbled himself in a limited human form in which He needed to be taught lessons of human survival from limited humans such as Mary and Joseph. Jesus who was present at the very creation of the earth was willing to become limited by the laws of the earth. Certainly He had every right to honor and praise, and yet the Incarnation teaches the importance of not grasping after entitled rights or status. Instead the Incarnation teaches the power of a servant's love. The servant knows that serving God with humility allows the power of God to truly work in and through him or her.

To love as God has called us to love is to take risks. When we respond to the great commandment with all of our hearts, we are made vulnerable. We are committing ourselves to loving neighbors who are not necessarily ready to receive our love and certainly not always able to appreciate our love. Servant love is not done out of any demand for reciprocation from the neighbor; it is given out of service to God with a prayer for our neighbor.

Where there is risk, there is natural resistance. Hence we need to be accountable to each other to move outside of our natural circles into the lives of people who may reject us or even seek to harm us. We build Christian enclaves to protect ourselves from outside dangers, but the reality is that the more we live to protect ourselves, the more we are vulnerable to the rejection and pain that comes from living in closed circles. Closed communities are inherently consumed by petty concerns because the focus becomes maintenance and self-preservation rather than a more dynamic call to mission. Even more importantly, when we close ourselves off from others, we miss out on the unknown miracles that would occur if we push ourselves out into the lives of others led by the Spirit of God. We are called to live by faith, which always demands a life that takes risks. The Christian life was never meant to be sedentary or routine. God calls us in every stage of life to be part of His new creation.

Service in the church obviously needs to be Spirit-driven, following the Spirit's moving, calling, and working power. Spirit-led service should mean that our lives are peppered with moments where we sense we're entering divine realms of significance. Too many of us have instead considered our service as a duty to be fulfilled. Why else would we hear in the halls of the church such things as, "I've served my time" or "I did that job for five years; it's someone else's turn." Certainly there is a season for certain types of service. We may often be part of a ministry because of our own stage of life. For example, there may be times when we are involved in preschool ministries because our children are young, not because we necessarily have a passion for that ministry. We can also be involved in a ministry for a period of time and sense that God is calling us to invest our time in another area. It is appropriate to make room for others in some areas of leadership and service. However, the problem is not so much that people stopped doing *something* but that they stopped doing anything. It is as if they saw themselves fulfilling some service contract. When we are talking about servanthood that participates in the transforming power of God, we should be celebrating new opportunities and new callings rather than reflecting on fulfilled obligations and expectations met.

Dallas Willard says, "In service we engage our goods and strength in the active promotion of the good of others and the causes of God in our world."[2] There is great beauty in participating in the causes of God in our world. We do not always see the immediate results, but we are participating in the larger movements of God's hovering, re-creating Spirit. It is as simple as engaging our resources to be the light in the darkness, hope for the despairing, and food for the hungry. The Christian Church should be known for its generosity and quick response to community needs. There have always been significant segments of the Christian community that have founded hospitals, cared for prisoners, housed the homeless, and fed the hungry. What is needed is a wider number of us to embrace this call in both small and large endeavors.

Along with the great commandment to love (and thus serve) is the Great Commission. We know we are to go into the world and make disciples. Nevertheless, we struggle with the actual realization of that goal. Again we have obstacles—old models that need to be broken and risk factors that need to be overcome. We need practical avenues through which we can join God in the work He is already doing in the hearts and lives of people all around us.

The Scriptures are filled with both directives and examples relating to our call to fulfill the Great Commission. The words of Christ found in Matt. 28:19 serve as the primary mission statement of the Church: "Therefore go and make disciples of all nations, baptizing them in the name of the Father and of the Son and of the Holy Spirit." We are told that the "son of man came to seek and save what was lost" (Luke 19:10). We have the model of Christ's life, which was involved in caring for both the spiritual and physical needs of the people He met. The great parables found in Luke 15 are foundational to our deepening call to seek out those who are lost. These stories of a lost sheep, a lost coin, and lost sons explicate for us the profound desire of God that all would be found and brought home. They also represent a God who seeks, searches, goes to great lengths, waits with a yearning heart, and even faces dangers to find the sheep, reclaim the coin, and embrace the son.

There are many excellent books on evangelism that encourage us to join in the already existing conversation occurring in every person's heart with God. Such books as *Becoming a Contagious Christian* by Bill Hybels and Mark Mittelberg,[3] *Out of the Saltshaker* by Rebecca Manley Pippert,[4] and *Gentle Persuasion* by Joe Aldrich[5] teach us to let God flow through us in a relational evangelism. We have often been trained to verbally run roughshod over people and start conversations with little or no understanding that there are "prefaith" conversations occurring in their hearts. We also often act as functional atheists—as if it were up to us alone to bring a person to faith. The doctrine of prevenient grace teaches us that God is already at work in people's hearts and lives. We can be guided by the Spirit to join in that ongoing conversation. This does not preclude help in discovering ways to present the gospel at the right time. The themes from those who teach relational evangelism encourage us to build on existing relationships, to make room in our lives for new relationships outside the church, and to make a commitment to willingly share in a real and relevant way how God is at work in our lives. These are significant ideas for the church to embrace. We have to continue to be challenged to build bridges to those outside our faith communities. If not, we will quickly become inward focused and begin to settle into the less risky activity of maintenance. It just seems to be our natural bent.

Both the call to service and the call to evangelism—usually separate programs in the local church—can be combined in the call to servant evangelism. A commitment to servant evangelism encourages the people of God to fulfill the great commandment and Great Commission. Tom Nees calls this "compassion evangelism."[6] He has shown significant leadership in challenging the church, particularly the Church of the Nazarene, to broaden the scope of her mission, widen the arms of her embrace, and ask the difficult questions regarding justice inside and outside the church. Ron Sider, who has been a proponent for engagement in issues of social justice among Evangelicals, refers to this as a combination of evangelism and social passion.[7] His has been a consistent voice that continues to be Evangelical in commitment but firm in its insistence that we are called to be a people concerned with justice. He describes this beautifully when he says, "I long for the time when most Christians are in congregations where each month they experience the joy of hearing about new people who have just begun to taste the goodness of salvation. I yearn for the day when most Christians are in congregations that walk with the needy, say no to all forms of prejudice, and reach out to heal broken communities."[8]

Steve Sjogren, the founding pastor of the Vineyard Church in Cincinnati, has led the way exploring, defining, and implementing a model of servant evangelism. There are churches that embody the ideas of servant evangelism without having a specific name or even a plan. These churches come in all sizes and are found in all kinds of places. They are the churches that have embraced the dual call to be people of compassion and evangelism. The power of God's Spirit and good leadership have made this part of their DNA. These churches have been able to combine the best qualities of two movements—the social gospel movement's concerns for justice and compassion and the church growth movement's commitment to worldwide evangelism. While in Scripture these commitments go hand in hand, some churches have chosen to emphasize one over the other, often with the loss of the "other."

Servant evangelism is not a list of things to do in a certain way. Each local church body will have to discover the areas of need in their communities to which they can respond. Some churches will invest in providing such ongoing services as food, education, and crisis counseling. Others may combine outreach with simple acts of service that let their communities know there is a God who cares and hears. Steve Sjogren's writings and web site[9] continue to reflect his commitment to encourage servant evangelism in the life of the church. He gives a functional definition of servant evangelism. He says it is "Demonstrating God's love by offering to do some humble act of service with no strings attached."[10]

The goal of servant evangelism is to get us out into the world. It is a simple approach that has lower risk factors than most outreach events. The church is simply surprising people with acts of love. This then can open the door to deeper conversations regarding issues of faith or pave the way for future conversations. Committing time, finances, and people to the lives of others in the community will at the least broaden our perspective on what church life can and should be. Perhaps if more of us embraced this way of being church, we would spend less time arguing over the color of carpets and more time celebrating that the blind have gained sight and the lost have been found.

I remember talking with a pastor friend about his church's plans for outreach. He told me he had discovered that more ripples were created by consistently throwing pebbles into a pond instead of one big expensive rock. We need to find ways to make our involvement in the community be consistent rather than sporadic. A consistent witness creates a reputation that lets people in the community know this church—this group of people—care. I remember standing in the foyer of our church on the opening night of a children's program geared to the community. The special needs of the children always caused this program to be a bit chaotic, and this certainly caused the staff some stress. However, one day one of the neighborhood women brought in a friend with her children. As she walked through the doors, she turned to her friend and said, "They really like our children here!" And with added surprise she said, "They want them to come." Such comments helped put our "stress" into proper perspective.

My husband and I are on a journey with our new church, a journey of discovery as we seek to be a people committed to servant evangelism. It is not an easy transition to make, and the jury is still out about whether being servant evangelists will become a primary identity of our people. It takes time to see if a core value really begins to saturate every aspect of who we are as a church. However, already, I am seeing great benefits coming from this investment. No, numbers are not flocking in, though as we are consistent in our acts of love and outreach, I expect to see some numerical response. The more immediate result is in the opening of our hearts to others—the breaking down of barriers between those of us who gather in the church and those who do not. Every time we step out in faith, we grow deeper and stronger.

One night I was out shopping with some families who needed some help with school supplies. As they began to thank me for the help, at first I said, "It wasn't me; it was the church," but then I corrected my statement. I said, "It wasn't the church; it's God. It's God who cares about you and your situation; it's God who sent us to show you a practical expression of His love." We have a great opportunity to join in the stream of God's communication already at work in the lives of those around us. What might it mean to a person who just that morning prayed "Are You there, God?" to have someone show up at his or her kid's game, hand them a bottle of water, and say, "This is a practical expression of God's love"?

We know in our own lives that when we begin to hear repeated themes, we wonder if God might be speaking to us. We pray about a mission trip, and all of a sudden everywhere we turn that trip's destination is mentioned. As a result we believe this new direction in our lives is confirmed. I know that God is speaking to the hearts of the people around me. If we as Christians begin to be consistent with our love and outreach, these people will hear repeated themes of a God who loves them and whom they can get to know through the people called Christians.

There are people outside the church wondering where they can go to explore issues of spirituality. They, for various reasons, explore all sorts of spiritual venues before considering the church. In this postmodern world limitless options exist outside of the Christian faith, and a general suspicion of most religious institutions encourages many to look for "spiritual" life elsewhere. When we stay inside our churches and demand that the rest of the world figure out we have something valuable to offer, we are creating unnecessary barriers between them and the good news of the gospel. If instead we surprise them by being a visible presence all over their towns—serving water, raking leaves, washing windows, or showing love in other practical ways—there is an increased likelihood that they might consider the way of Jesus Christ. They might realize that the church down the street cares about them enough to walk out to where they are. We become a "go to" church rather than a "come to" church. We, by the power of the Holy Spirit, take the first steps to those outside the community of faith, just as God took the first step toward us.

It is so easy as pastor and church member to have all of our time chewed up by programs, problems, and issues inside the church walls. We can be like hamsters on an exercise wheel, all out of breath and going nowhere. However, by our ongoing, steady commitment to be people who venture out to do acts of servant evangelism, we may find fresh breath as we forge into new territory.

For the people who commit to this venture, there are multiple rewards. They begin to experience a greater sense of community as they head out on adventures with others from their churches, they have new opportunities to see what God might want to do through their lives, and they find themselves sharing in a mission that is larger than they had previously known. The deepening sense of community creates a momentum for an ongoing commitment to both service and evangelism.

A common desire in the church is the yearning to belong. In every church I have served people have complained about their sense of isolation; they desire to feel accepted, loved, and appreciated. A church can make itself crazy trying to assuage this need by communicating love, extending itself with multiple touch points, and assuring people of their acceptance. Certainly this is a legitimate need. However, those who have difficulties experiencing love and acceptance will usually find themselves cared for much better by becoming involved in serving others. Not only does their focus begin to shift off their own felt needs, but they also develop a deeper bond with those serving with them.

More significantly, engagement in servant evangelism is an obedient action to God's invitation. We begin to be about something bigger than maintenance. We begin to be about mission and meaning.

One thing that discourages people from being involved in this type of service is fear. They are afraid of being put in embarrassing situations.

We can alleviate this fear by admitting that these kinds of feelings are normal and by talking about how we are lowering the embarrassment quotient. We can also assure them that they will be sent out in groups. People are also afraid of being tricked. Unfortunately churches have sometimes been less than honest about the time commitment a ministry will demand or the full story of its nature. We need to be honest with people about the amount of time required as well as what kind of experience they might expect. When we head out to engage in servant evangelism, some groups may be raking while others are delivering baked goods to unsuspecting police or firefighters, offering free tutoring, or serving the homeless. There can be great joy in each of those activities. The joy is diminished if a person signs up to be involved in one experience and it gets switched without any guilt-free way to back out. If they show up expecting a two-hour commitment and end up having their whole day chewed up, you can be sure they will not be back again. Even at the lower-risk level of this type of evangelism, there is still trepidation.

The reality is that we will feel uneasy when we take steps out of our comfort zones toward others. But think how much more difficult it is for someone who has never been in church to make those steps toward us. Who should be the first to step out? Who should take the first risk? Those of us who have been sent out by Christ must overcome our propensity for comfort. Take an easy assignment as your first step. Stop by the police department with a basket of muffins or a plate of cookies and watch what happens when you inform them that this is a "practical expression of God's love." They might look at you as if you are the strangest person to walk in that door, or they might begin a new spiritual adventure. Either way, you have entered into the life of another in a life-altering way. The effectiveness of this outreach is not only the people you directly touch but also all the people they will tell about your crazy church that gave them free bottles of water.

There is great strength in numbers. As we head out together, we are emboldened by the company. We can celebrate together as we recognize what God can do when His people begin to reach by faith beyond the walls of the church in acts of love and mercy.

As pastors and leaders of our local churches, we need to make room within our churches for an ongoing commitment to servant evangelism. We must be convinced and able to convince others that fulfilling the great commandment and the Great Commission really is the primary mission of the church. We as the church must no longer be satisfied with just having a good time together and taking care of each other. We must not be like the rich man Lazarus, who feasted while the beggar died of hunger. We must be about fulfilling our call—about being a people who are Christlike. Christ cried over the city that was lost, looked at people outside the religious community with love, and sought to bring good news to all. It is ultimately a self-serving commitment to be a people who are servant evangelists. For the life of compassion is the abundant life God desires to give us. It is the choice between being a stagnant pond or a flowing river of life.

Notes

1. Thomas Nees, *Compassion Evangelism: Meeting Human Needs* (Kansas City: Beacon Hill Press of Kansas City, 1996), 55.

2. Dallas Willard, *The Spirit of the Disciplines: Understanding How God Changes Lives* (New York: HarperCollins, 1988), 182.

3. Bill Hybels and Mark Mittelberg, *Becoming a Contagious Christian* (Grand Rapids: Zondervan, 1994).

4. Rebecca Manley Pippert, *Out of the Saltshaker and into the World* (Downers Grove, Ill.: InterVarsity Press, 1979).

5. Joe Aldrich, *Gentle Persuasion* (Portland, Oreg.: Multnomah, 1988).

6. Nees, *Compassion Evangelism: Meeting Human Needs*, 19.

7. Ronald Sider, *Living like Jesus: Eleven Essentials for Growing a Genuine Faith* (Grand Rapids: Baker Book House Co., 1999), 98.

8. Ibid.

9. Steve Sjogren's web site: www.servantevangelism.com

10. Steve Sjogren, *Conspiracy of Kindness: A Refreshing Approach to Sharing the Love of Jesus with Others* (Ann Arbor, Mich.: Vine Books, 1993), 17.

Kennon L. Callahan, Ph.D.—pastor, researcher, and professor—is today's most sought-after church consultant and speaker. He has worked with thousands of congregations around the world and has helped tens of thousands of church leaders and pastors. His dynamic seminars are filled with wisdom and encouragement, practical possibilities, and helpful suggestions.

Author of many books, he is best known for his groundbreaking *Twelve Keys to an Effective Church,* which has formed the basis for a widely acclaimed Mission Growth Movement that is helping congregations across the planet.

Dr. Callahan has earned the B.A., M.Div., S.T.M., and Ph.D. degrees; his doctorate is in systematic theology. He has served as a pastor of rural and urban congregations in Ohio, Texas, and Georgia. He taught for many years at Emory University.

His newest book is *The Future That Has Come.* Other recent books include *Twelve Keys for Living, A New Beginning for Pastors and Congregations,* and *Small Strong Congregations.*

He and his wife, Julia, grew up in Cuyahoga Falls, Ohio. They have two sons, Ken and Mike, and three grandchildren. They enjoy the outdoors, hiking, horseback riding, camping, music, sailing, and quilting.

10

Sacrament and Cloud

Kennon L. Callahan

GRACE

❧ A VISIT IS A SIGN OF GRACE. IT IS LIKE A SACRAMENT—an outer and visible sign of an inner and spiritual grace. A visit is an act of sharing healing and wholeness. It is a time of joy and wonder: The lives of two persons share grace, compassion, community, hope.

A visit has its own integrity and value. It's neither a sales technique nor a means to an end. We visit as an expression of the Incarnation, as a way of sharing the mission.

Visiting is central to the experience of the Christian movement. God himself is a visitor.

> Praise to the Lord, the God of Israel, for he has visited
> and redeemed his people (*Luke 1:68, see* KJV).

Sometimes we've become preoccupied with the part of the text that says God has redeemed His people. The text is clear. God is not some distant, far-off, nebulous entity. Our God is the God who has *visited* His people. J. B. Phillips once wrote a play titled *The Visited Planet,* telling of Christ as the greatest visit of all.

God visits to redeem. God visits, then redeems, and not from afar. God's visit with us has a sacramental character, just as ours on behalf of God's mission do. Visiting is the key with which many people open the door to relationship with God, to meaning and hope for their lives.

As a sacramental act, a visit is among the deepest, most visible expressions of grace that people share with one another. One person seeks out another person for the sake of sharing good news. God's grace is present in the visit.

By God's own action, God has shown us that visiting is what He invites us to do. That God has visited His people is an amazing gift. Among all the things God might have done, it is astonishing, extraordinary, unheard of, that God would visit with us.

In going out to share Christ, we discover Christ. Jesus said,

Lo, I am with you alway (*Matt. 28:20, KJV*).

Jesus invites the disciples to Go. Then He assures them of His presence with them. It is in the going that we discover the presence of Christ. It is not accidental that the invitation to Go occurs first; then the assurance comes. We find Christ in the midst of the world. When we stay "inside," we wither and decay.

Christ wanted the disciples to know where they would find His presence—in the world. Christ wants us to know that in visiting we will discover His compassion and hope, the strength of His presence and assurance, the power of His love and grace.

I'm suggesting that your visit is like sharing a sacrament. You are surrounded by a sacred spirit when you visit. There is a genuine sense in which God is richly and fully present in it.

A visit, finally, is not our own doing. It is a gift of God. We receive as we share. Christ, in His wisdom, knows that the great good news of joy and wonder, compassion and hope, is received as it is shared. If not shared, it wastes away. Christ shares His grace with us in our visiting, and we discover Him as we share Him.

COMPASSION

A visit is a sign of compassion. Visiting is not a matter of duty or obligation. Please don't go visiting out of a sense of dutiful commitment. You won't be at your best. The visit won't be at its best. You won't be helpful in people's lives.

Those who visit best see a visit as an expression of sharing and caring, love and concern. Through visiting, people share their faith in deeds as well as in words. Compassion sharing is as helpful as faith sharing. Deeds of compassion speak as strongly as words. A visit is a deed of compassion.

People who visit with a compelling sense of compassion are more interested in how they can help than in what words they should say. Their compassion gives them the words that are needed and helps them focus the visit with the person being visited.

Compassion is foundational to healthy relationships. Kids care about what the teacher knows because they know the teacher cares. The team plays well for the coach because they know the coach cares for the team. The family pulls together when there is a genuine spirit of compassion.

Compassion runs. It doesn't wait in the house for the young son to draw nigh. Compassion doesn't walk slowly and begrudgingly toward the young son. Compassion runs.

In Luke 15:20, we discover these words:

And when the young son was yet a long way off, his father saw him and had compassion and he ran to him (*see NIV*).

The text does not say, "And while his young son was yet a long way off, the father saw him and waited in the house."

The text does not say, "And while the young son was yet a long way off, the father saw him and walked slowly, begrudgingly."

What the text says is, The father had *compassion* and he *ran* to him.

Compassion runs. Compassion doesn't wait or walk. Compassion is not a matter of waiting for people in your community to show up in church. It is not a matter of slowly, begrudgingly walking to them, as though they should have had an interest and showed up on their own. Compassion runs to persons in the community and shares with them the richness of God's compassion.

God runs to us with compassion. God has shown us how to run with compassion. God invites us to run with compassion.

COMMUNITY

A visit is a sign of community. From ancient times until today, and throughout the planet, an important custom has been the extension of genuine hospitality to strangers. When the stranger approaches and is invited into the campfire circle, the hosts offer an almost sacred welcome. There is the sense that, for this moment, we are community with one another.

When we visit, we express our interest in community. We're not visiting simply to get information or to give information. We're not visiting primarily to get members. In these days of isolation and insulation, of loneliness and despair, we visit to express our solidarity, our sense of community, with one another.

People are desperately searching for community. For many people their sense of community has been broken. Our visits with them are genuine gestures of community. We will visit with people who are scared, scarred, cold, indifferent, angry. What else could one expect in a world where family and community structures have collapsed all around?

As you visit, think of your best friends. You'll be amazed at how many new best friends you'll discover in your visits. Remember also those with whom you have found a sense of community. You'll be amazed at the sense of community you'll both discover and share in your visits.

HOPE

Our hope is in God. Civilizations rise and fall. Empires come and go. The mission of God is eternal. It endures, and it is where our hope lies. A visit is a sign of mission, a sign of hope.

We visit because God first visited us. In the New Testament we discover these words:

> We love, because he first loved us (*1 John 4:19*, RSV).

Christ comes to us. He doesn't wait for us. Christ visits us to share His compassion and hope, and we visit in the same spirit—to share the Good News.

The purpose of our visiting is mission growth, not church growth. There are a few who have said that visiting no longer works. But they have in mind that it no longer works to achieve church growth. That misses the point.

The purpose is mission. Visiting works for mission. Visiting may or may not work for membership growth. The point is, in visiting, people's lives are helped in the name of Christ. God calls us to a theology of service, not a theology of survival. The purpose of visiting is mission growth, discipleship growth. Someone once asked me, "Is evangelism the answer to church growth?" That is the wrong question.

We're not called to be preoccupied with the survival of an institution. God calls us to be preoccupied with the lives and destinies of persons in the name of Christ.

These are more helpful questions:
- Is visiting the answer to mission growth?
- Is visiting the answer to discipleship growth?
- Do we live out mission and evangelism in our visiting?
- Do people discover compassion and hope in visiting?

The answer to these questions is *Yes.*

God gives His Son freely, without obligation. A gift is a gift when there is no obligation. God visits us that we might discover grace, compassion, community, hope.

The church is called to be *in* the world but not *of* the world. The church's identity is *in* the world. Jesus prayed to God,

> As thou didst send me into the world,
> so I have sent them into the world (*John 17:18*, RSV).

We visit freely, without obligation. We visit as a gift. A gift with an obligation isn't a gift. We don't visit to obligate people but to offer the gifts of grace, compassion, community, and hope. God shows us the way. We visit because God first visits us, and God is our hope.

CLOUDS OF WITNESSES

Our lives are surrounded by a great cloud of witnesses. As we visit, we are surrounded by this cloud of witnesses. The mission of the Christian movement is never individualistic. No one visits alone.

Therefore, since we are surrounded by so great a cloud of
witnesses, . . . let us run with unflinching purpose the
race that is set before us, looking unto Jesus (*Heb. 12:1, see* RSV).

This cloud of witnesses is made up of our mentors, encouragers, nurturers, coaches, cheerleaders, and of all who have visited on behalf of the Christian movement since the time of Christ. They go with us as we visit.

Christ is with you. The disciples are with you. Paul is there with you. The missionaries of the Early Church, who carried the Christian gospel to the far corners of the world, are there with you. Augustine, Thomas, Francis, Luther, Calvin—these and many more are with you.

Across the centuries, people who have gone visiting have sensed the presence of all these witnesses—known and unknown—with them as they visit. They are there to encourage you; try to sense their presence as you visit.

We don't visit alone. We go in the company of all who have gone before and who will follow—sharing God's compassion and grace, peace and hope, with those in the community. They give us confidence that our visits hold promise for people's lives and destinies.

Throughout the history of Christianity, there have been important times when visiting in the community has been central to the movement. This is one of those times. Go. Visit well in the name of God. Let us run with unflinching purpose the race that is set before us. Look unto Jesus.

This chapter is reprinted from *Visiting in an Age of Mission*, chap. 17, by Kennon L. Callahan, copyright © 1994 by Kennon L. Callahan. This material is used by permission of John Wiley & Sons, Inc.

Adam Hamilton is senior pastor and the founding pastor of the Church of the Resurrection in Leawood, Kansas. He earned an undergraduate degree from Oral Roberts University, Tulsa, Oklahoma, and a master of divinity degree from the Perkins School of Theology at Southern Methodist University, Dallas, in 1988. In previous assignments he has served as youth minister and associate pastor in charge of evangelism. He now leads one of the three most dynamic and rapidly growing congregations in the United Methodist denomination, a congregation that has grown in 13 years from less than 100 to more than 12,000 adult members and children. Adam currently serves as a trustee of Saint Paul School of Theology in Kansas City. He also serves as a member of the Large Church Initiative Steering Committee for the United Methodist Church.

Adam received the Circuit Rider award in 1996. This award is presented annually by the United Methodist Publishing House for overall excellence in ministry. In 2000 Adam was named one of the "Ten People to Watch" in shaping the country's spiritual landscape by *Religion and Ethics Newsweekly*. The Foundation for Evangelism recognized Adam as the Distinguished Evangelist of The United Methodist Church for the year 2000. He has been awarded two honorary doctorates. Adam has authored three books published by Abingdon Press: *Confronting the Controversies: A Christian Looks at the Tough Issues; Leading Beyond the Walls: Developing Mainline Congregations with a Heart for the Unchurched;* and *Unleashing the Word: Preaching with Relevance, Purpose, and Passion.*

11

Effective Follow-up Strategies

Adam Hamilton

❧ FREQUENTLY PEOPLE ASK ME WHAT WE DID WHEN OUR CHURCH was just starting that was most important to its later growth and success. I quickly answer by mentioning five things: (1) prayer, (2) developing and communicating our values and vision, (3) marketing, (4) preaching, and (5) effectively following up on new visitors. In this article I would like to focus on No. 5—the pastor's role in effective evangelistic follow-up. But first let me tell you a story.

When I was in college, I sold women's shoes for an upscale department store to pay my tuition. There were just two of us selling these shoes—Pearl Golden and me. Pearl was in her 60s and was a kind Christian woman. She had been selling women's shoes in this department for years. She was not the epitome of fashion—she wore only the most comfortable of shoes. She looked more like a grandmother than a fashion consultant, but when it came to selling shoes, she was outstanding.

On her day off I would stand in the shoe department, and women would walk in, look around, and then ask, "Is Pearl here today?" I would say, "No, today is her day off, but I would love to help you." I would inevitably hear the same words, "Oh, that's OK, I'll come back tomorrow when Pearl is back." As a poor college student working on commission, I hated those words. After several months of trying to understand why so many women insisted on having Pearl help them, I finally asked her, "Pearl, what is your secret?" She said, "Every time I sell a pair of shoes, after the customer leaves, I sit down and write a personal thank-you note to them." Over the years this small effort had paid huge dividends, and Pearl had built a base of very loyal customers.

By the time I took my first youth director's position, at a small church in Bixby, Oklahoma, I had already adopted and been practicing

Pearl's art of shoe-selling follow-up. Now working with teens, I applied what I had learned. Every time a young person would visit our youth fellowship, I would get his or her name and address. The next day after school I would drop by the teen's home and leave a small gift and a note thanking the teen for visiting our youth program. The youth group grew from 13 kids on my first Sunday to 36 kids 11 months later when I graduated from college.

I used this same strategy at New World United Methodist Church in Dallas, where I served as youth director while in seminary. In just over three years, attendance grew almost tenfold. Something similar happened in my first pastoral appointment out of seminary, where I served as an associate pastor at Central United Methodist Church—a 150-year-old congregation in the heart of Kansas City. A team of laypeople and I divided up the altar flowers each week and delivered them to our first-time visitors on Sunday afternoon. In about two years this church saw growth in both membership and worship attendance at a rate it had not seen in 20 years.

So when my wife and I started the United Methodist Church of the Resurrection in 1990, I knew that follow-up would be an important part of our plans. We started out by delivering coffee mugs with the church's name on them to each first-time visitor. Back then only a few churches in the United States were doing this—today this is fairly commonplace.

Each Sunday during worship we would pass attendance notebooks down the rows and draw attention to them periodically during the service. We would ask the congregants to look at what people wrote so they could identify and welcome their seatmates by name after the service (this activity dramatically increased the number of persons actually leaving their names and addresses). After worship was over, I would look in the notebooks for every first-time visitor and write his or her name and address on a visitation card. Later, after lunch, I would drop by, unannounced, for a doorstep visit.

These visits were always very short. When the individual came to the door, he or she often looked at me with an expression that said, "I knew I shouldn't have left my name and address!" But I would quickly put the person at ease, saying, "I don't want to come in; I just wanted to drop by for a moment to give you this coffee mug from our church—it is a sign of our welcome. I also wanted you to know how glad we are that you visited this morning. We really hope you come back!" After this I would ask if the person had any questions about the church. If not, I would say, "Again, thank you for visiting this morning. I hope to see you next Sunday!" The average visit took just under four minutes. But this was an important four minutes.

Because I had written the name of the individual down on the visitor card and actually stopped by his or her home for a visit, I was able to recall that person's name later at the next worship service. When I could call a person walking into worship by name, that person was hooked! To remember someone's name communicates that you think he or she is important. Recently I walked into a restaurant and the waitress called me by name, and as I sat down, she brought me my favorite soft drink. This small act made me feel as if I was a special customer, and it made me want to return again and again. Remembering people's names really does make a difference.

I've known pastors who send letters and make telephone calls to new visitors, and I think this is good. But a doorstep visit allows you to get to know your visitors and communicates to them a level of welcome that they will not receive in a note or telephone call. During the first four years of our church's existence I delivered 800 coffee mugs to first-time visitors. In the early years this took less than an hour of my time each week—but it was an incredibly important hour.

If the truth were known, most of us pastors are filled with dread at the thought of doing this. I would become anxious at first when I would deliver the mugs. I would secretly hope the people weren't home so I could just leave them a note in the mug by their door. But once I got in the habit of doing it, I came to enjoy it. It was a blessing to me. I no longer do this ministry in our church. Today we have a team of dedicated laypeople who deliver between 50 and 100 coffee mugs to first-time visitors each week. We call these visitors our "Methodist Muggers." They do a fabulous job. When your church reaches a certain size, you will need to turn this over to laypeople. But as long as a pastor can keep up with this on his or her own, I believe it to be a valuable part of developing dynamic congregations and effectively reaching the unchurched.

What I've described was the first prong of our two-pronged approach to following up on new visitors. The second would happen three weeks after the first visit. Each week I would track a visitor's attendance. On the third visit I would phone the visitor and say, "Hello, this is Adam Hamilton from the Church of the Resurrection. I am so excited that you've been worshiping with us each week! One of my aims is to get to know all of the people who worship with us on the weekend, and

I was wondering if I could come by one night this week to get to know you better and answer any questions you have about the church. I won't stay more than 45 minutes, as I'll have another visit after yours. Would that be OK?"

Notice I did not ask the person if he or she wanted me to come over. If I had, the person would probably say no so as not to inconvenience me or take time away from my family. But because I expressed a desire to come over, in essence invited myself, the person would probably not turn me down, and very few did.

When I arrived for this visit, I would thank the person again for allowing me to do this, and then I would ask questions about his or her life. I found that most people enjoyed talking about themselves and telling their stories, but in today's world, no one wants to listen. When I would listen and express interest, this was a blessing to the people I would meet and to me. It helped me to connect with them and to love them.

After hearing the person's story, I would ask if it was OK if I told mine. I would then share a brief summary of my life, including my conversion experience. I did not do this to preach or especially witness to the person but just to share my story, including the most important part of my life—my walk with Christ.

Before I left, I would share with the person a bit of the vision of our church, and our expectations for membership (for more on this see my book *Leading Beyond the Walls*, Abingdon Press, 2002). Finally I would tell how honored I would be to be the person's pastor. I would end our time together by asking if I could pray for the person and his or her family. This was a unique opportunity in that most unchurched people have never had another adult pray aloud with them. Because I had heard the person's story, I knew a bit about what I ought to be praying. I cannot tell you the number of times I would look up at the end of this prayer and see tears streaming down the face of the one for whom I was praying. In that moment of prayer, I had become his or her pastor.

Of the 400 plus households I visited in this way during those early years of our church's history, 399 of them joined the church. But more than simply becoming new members, these persons became very supportive of my leadership and of the church. I had taken the time to get to know them, to actually come to their homes (twice—the coffee mug visit and the in-home visit), to hear their stories, and to pray with them. This was a small investment in their lives that paid tremendous dividends in my ministry and for the church.

One thing you will notice—my aim on the second visit was not to lead them to Christ that night. If they wished to commit their lives to Christ, I would gladly lead them in prayer to do so. But most of our new visitors were not at the point where they were ready to do this. Instead I would be gently leading them toward Christ by sharing my faith story, praying with them, and inviting them to continue to be actively involved in the church. I was developing a relationship with them so I could continue to lead and disciple them in the weeks and months ahead in worship. Nearly all these persons ultimately did commit their lives to Christ. But had I pressured them to make this decision on the night of my visit, I would have pushed them away from Christ rather than gently leading them to Him.

Today committed laypeople deliver our coffee mugs, and with over 100 adults joining the church each month, I no longer visit each family in their home. We have a monthly gathering, our "Coffee with the Pastors," during which we try to re-create some of the same connection we had with our visitors in those early years. In this way we continue to pursue the same principles we used at the start. But this does not begin to have the same impact as the in-home pastoral visits did. I am convinced that the doorstep visits and the in-home visits were foundational for all that God would do through our church in the years ahead.

For Further Reading

Many of the leadership books I have most enjoyed in the last few years were not written specifically for churches. Here are a few of my favorites.

Collins, Jim. *Good to Great*. New York: HarperCollins, 2001.
Frankl, Viktor. *Man's Search for Meaning*. New York: Pocket Books, 1946.
Johnson, C. Ray. *CEO Logic*. Franklin Lakes, N.J.: Career Press, 1998.
Kotter, John. *Leading Change*. Boston: Harvard Business School Press, 1996.

Tom Theriault, D.Min., currently serves as associate pastor for mission and outreach at the Solana Beach Presbyterian Church, Solana Beach, California (in north San Diego County). A congregation of over 1,600 members, Solana Beach Presbyterian supports a wide range of mission activities, including the support of missionaries around the world and a food truck ministry that handles some 10 million pounds of food a year. Dr. Theriault has spearheaded his church's commitment to plant the gospel among a group of Muslims in the Ethiopian desert and is very involved in the expansion of the congregation's ministry to Hispanics. He also chairs the mission committee of the Presbytery of San Diego, leading these 35 congregations to make a commitment to frontier missions.

Dr. Theriault earned his doctorate from the School of World Mission at Fuller Theological Seminary, doing research on the topic "The Influence of Universalism in Presbyterian Mission Policy and Practice in the 20th Century." He and his wife have three children—Anna, Julie, and Steve—a wonderful son-in-law, and an adorable grandson.

12

A Globally Engaged Church

Tom Theriault

A PRELIMINARY CONFESSION

I MUST ADMIT TO BEING A JOHNNY-COME-LATELY TO MISSIONS.
For the first two-thirds of my Christian walk and the first third of my vocational ministry, I was essentially clueless about the Great Commission. Oh, I believed in missions. After all, I was a Bible-believing Evangelical. I was eager to lead people to Christ and loved to disciple people in Christ. But truthfully, I had little knowledge of and almost no involvement in what God was doing in the world beyond my own American middle-class culture.

Missions was very much a closet concern for me and for the churches I served. We paid lip service to missions, but mission matters were kept in the closet and dusted off for our annual mission conference, seldom to be heard about for the rest of the year. We imagined a spiritually dynamic church to be one that was winning its neighbors to Christ and providing challenging programs to grow them in Christ. Yet the Great Commission insists, "Go . . . and make disciples of all nations, . . . and lo, I am with you always" (Matt. 28:19-20, RSV). It turns out that the *promise* of Christ's presence is stubbornly attached to His *command* to "go." One great mission leader, Ralph Winter, likes to quip, "No 'go,' no 'lo'!"

In my own life, I have discovered that when I go, when I step outside my comfortable ruts and routines and dare to become involved in Christ's global purposes, *that* is when the power and presence of Christ are most unforgettable. I have discovered the same holds true for the saints I have been privileged to shepherd. Whether we are building Habitat for Humanity houses in a depressed part of our city or lifting up the name of Christ among those in other lands, again and again I have seen ordinary believers meet an extraordinary Savior when they robustly dive into the work of accomplishing God's saving purposes in the world. When a congregation is populated with such "get up and go" be-lievers, it will be truly dynamic with Christ's presence!

THE GOSPEL: MORE THAN M & M'S?

I look back on my first 10 years of pastoral ministry and now realize I was promoting a dangerously reduced gospel. It was the gospel I was given as an unsaved high schooler and the gospel I was giving away as an enthusiastic youth pastor. I like to refer to this domesticated salva-tion as the "M & M gospel," the More & More for Me & Mine gospel—the "What can you do for me today, God?" gospel.

This is the gospel I was earnestly passing along to the youth I served. I longed to connect them with Jesus so that He would be included in every part of their lives: their peer relationships, their family ties, their career aspirations, even their sex lives! Borrowing a commercial jingle of the day, I wanted to persuade them that "things go better with Christ."

As true as this certainly is, it is not true enough. It reduces the God of the universe to a celestial bellhop whose main job and occupation is to help *me*, heal *me*, and make *my* life hum along a little better. This gospel sets us up for a deadly fall. It effectively places me at the center of the universe and assigns to God the job of serving me, of making my life happier. In our razzle-dazzle Sunday Schools and youth groups we unwit-tingly convince kids that the chief aim of life is to be happy and enter-tained (after all, even God's main ambition is to cater to our needs). And then we send them out into a world where there are endless de-structive avenues that promise happiness and entertainment. No won-der "surveys reveal little difference between church attenders and non-attenders in the rates of premarital intercourse and cohabitation."[1]

Please don't get me wrong. I love M & M's. In fact, I hope the streets of heaven are not paved with gold; M & M cobblestones sound more inviting to me! M & M's are great as a snack but dangerous as a staple in our diet. If that is all you feed yourself, your body will suffer. Similarly, the M & M gospel is a precious part of the promise of salva-tion. Jesus does love, care about, and long to heal me and those around me. But if that M & M gospel is all I feed my faith and all I feed my church, my faith and the Body of Christ I serve will suffer. Our faith will be ingrown and anemic. When God is not Johnny-on-the-spot to help us the way we want, when prayers for our health and healing are not an-swered as we would like, our M & M faith fails. In stark contrast, how uplifting it was recently to listen to a brother who has been out and about in mission tell about the recurrence of his cancer. Instead of dwelling on dark doubts, he expressed a robust faith in a faithful God whom he had seen working redemptively in the hardships of Christians in Africa and Latin America.

The M & M gospel is a dangerously reduced version of the full-bodied, life-gripping call that the world heard from the lips of Jesus. "Come follow me and I'll transform you into something beyond your dreams. Your life will be turned inside out. You'll not be gobbling up goodies from God as much as you'll be pouring your life into God's global purposes of saving others." My wife, who directs the children's ministry in our church, likes to tell our kids that the gospel is "not just about getting Jesus into your heart; it's about getting you into the heart of Jesus." The full-throttled, hope-sustaining gospel is about getting me outside myself. It is about attaching my life's ambitions to something much greater and better than personal happiness and entertainment.

A few years ago when I was speaking about the M & M gospel, a young attorney observed, "You know, Tom, if you turn the M & M's upside down, you get W/W, a 'We are for the World' gospel!" It was 10 years into my pastoral ministry that I discovered this larger, more vigorous "We are for the World" gospel. It has changed my life, the way I do ministry, and the outlook and ambitions of the churches I have been privileged to serve. I count it an honor to pass along to you some of the insights that have transformed me and mine from M & M Christians to W/W disciples.

MISSION: MAINLINE OR SIDELINE

I'll never forget the meeting. The mission elder of a large church in our city came to my office for a visit. Doug was a young, visionary mission leader, and we had enjoyed many stimulating conversations about mission projects and strategies. I was therefore totally taken aback when he said, "Tom, I no longer think God wants missions to be part of the church." Doug let me hang in shock for a moment and then, with an impish twinkle in his eye, continued, "I don't think God wants missions to be part of the church; He wants it to be the *heart* of the church."

To put it another way, does God want His global mission to simply be a sideline in the church, one of many programs and causes competing for the time, attention, and budget of the Body? Or does He expect His worldwide purposes to occupy the mainline of the church's life, infusing every facet of ministry with a larger, more athletic vision and trajectory? In the past 15 years, I have come to see that the mission of Christ in the world is to be at the heart of the church because it is at the heart of

God. The God we meet in the Bible, from Genesis to Revelation, is a God whose heart beats with passion for all the peoples of the world. To be sure, He acts to save and sanctify His chosen people. But He saves and sanctifies them to *send* them into the world to take that redeeming love to those who have yet to hear and see it. When God's people get going and share this life-saving gospel, the blessings of that gospel abound for them and for the world. But when God's people are content to sit and soak in the blessings of the gospel, they risk having Him remove those blessings and forcefully export them to the world. This simple dynamic is one of the central themes tying God's Word together as a gripping drama of salvation.

Far from being an invention or afterthought of Jesus, the Great Commission pervades the entire Bible. And far from being the calling of a few supersaints, the mission of God in the world is given to all the people of God. All who are saved are sent; all who are converted are called. Every follower of Jesus is to follow Him into the world to play some strategic role in the saving of the nations. The roles will differ according to each one's gifts, but the calling is the same. This sacred calling sets the stage for the whole biblical drama.[2]

The Global Drama in the Old Testament

The very first line of the Bible strikes a missionary chord! What kind of a God do we find? John Stott makes the point vividly:

> We should never allow ourselves to forget that the Bible begins with the universe, not with the planet earth; then with the earth, not with Palestine; then with Adam the father of the human race, not with Abraham the father of the chosen race. Since, then, God is the Creator of the universe, the earth and all mankind, we must never demote him to the status of a tribal deity [an M & M God!]. Nor must we suppose that God chose Abraham and his descendants because he had lost interest in other peoples or given them up. Election is not a synonym for elitism.[3]

God struck an all-encompassing deal with Abraham and Sarah. Long before the Great Commission, God made the "go" of the gospel crystal clear: "Leave your country, your people and your father's household [three times God had to hammer home the call to leave the comfortable and cozy] and go" (Gen. 12:1). He then promised Abraham five blessings. The first four seem obviously desirable—land, reputation, offspring, and protection. What more could a wandering, childless couple hope for? God does care about our M & M concerns, about helping and healing us. But as Old Testament scholar Walter Kaiser notes, these blessings are "immediately followed by a purpose clause. It is 'so that you may be a blessing.' Not one of these promised blessings was to be for Abraham's self-aggrandizement" [the M & M mentality].[4]

The fifth blessing God promised was really the best of all. It was the one blessing that would keep the other four from destroying the people of God—"and all the peoples on earth will be blessed through you" (Gen. 12:3). In Gen. 11, God divided humanity into people groups and then chose one small people group, that of Abram and Sarai. He promised to bless them fully so that they might export the full blessings of salvation to all the other people groups. Kaiser puts it succinctly: "This man and his descendants were to be missionaries and channels of the truth from the beginning."[5]

The stage is set, the curtain parts, and the drama of the Bible unfolds. A missionary God seeks to reclaim a rebellious humanity by selecting one family to reach all the other families. So the question is, "Did God's chosen people sit and soak in the blessings of salvation, or did they get going and share those blessings with all the nations?"

When Jacob and his sons were in the Promised Land, God arranged for them, first through sibling rivalry and then through famine, to be relocated to Egypt. Jacob's son Joseph became an articulate missionary in the court of Pharaoh, interpreting the king's bad dreams in the name of Yahweh and gaining honor and high position. Four hundred years later when persecution replaced favor, God raised up Moses to deliver His people from Egyptian oppression. Yet the deliverance was itself to be a clear witness—"that my name might be proclaimed in all the earth" (Exod. 9:16). God delivers His people from oppression and depression because He loves them *and* wants to witness through them.

After dividing into two kingdoms, God's people in many ways abandoned their missionary call and turned inward, vying for territory and riches. The M & M mentality ran rampant. God sent prophets to plead with them to reclaim their missional purpose: "You are my servant, Israel, in whom I will display my splendor. . . . I will . . . make you a light for the Gentiles, that you may bring my salvation to the ends of the earth" (Isa. 49:3, 6). Yet, in general the people did not respond accordingly. In the story of Jonah we find typified their refusal to fulfill their global calling. When God talks about His mercy for Nineveh, Jonah sulks under a plant, more interested in losing the comfort of the plant's shade than in gaining the salvation of another people (chap. 4). Johannes Verkuyl quotes a clever poem by Thomas Carlisle:

Jonah stalked
to his shaded seat
and waited for God
to come around
to his way of thinking.
And God is still waiting for a host of Jonahs
in their comfortable houses
to come around
to his way of loving.[6]

The Global Drama in the New Testament

The hope of the people of Israel was fixed on their Messiah. What kind of hope rang loud in their heart—an M & M Messiah or a Messiah on the move? A sit-and-soak Savior or a Savior for the nations? Much to the dismay of the chosen people, the Man from Galilee had His heart set on all the peoples of the earth.

Matthew's Gospel spells this out with great clarity. Writing to a Jewish audience, Matthew wastes no time in revealing the global origins and appeal of the "Jewish" Messiah. In the genealogy, we find Matthew mentioning two pagan women, Rahab and Ruth, and a woman who was pagan by marriage, the wife of Uriah the Hittite (Bathsheba). This would have jarred any self-absorbed, Gentile-dismissing Jew of the day. How outrageous to imagine that the "Jewish" Savior was pleased to have pagan blood in His veins, that He came *from* the nations!

This long-awaited One also appealed *to* the nations. According to Matthew, the first ones to worship the newborn King (of the Jews?) were not the Jewish shepherds, as Luke tells the story, but the astrologers from the East! The star rose first in the east (not over Jerusalem), and some pagan stargazers responded in faith—unthinkable to a self-confined Jewish mind! As the drama of Jesus' ministry unfolds, Matthew ushers onstage a Roman officer (8:5-13) and a Syrian woman (15:21-28), whom Jesus congratulates for their "great faith," while chiding His own Jewish followers for the smallness of theirs. At the end of the story, while Jewish tongues are mocking the crucified Lord, a Gentile centurion exclaims, "Surely he was the Son of God!" (Matt. 27:54).

When Jesus foretold the birth of the Church, He described the secret of its dynamism. The Church will be empowered by the Holy Spirit, and any authentically Spirit-empowered Church *"will* be my witnesses in Jerusalem, and in all Judea [local mission], and Samaria and to the ends of the earth [cross-cultural/global mission]." Jesus promoted a Spirit-inspired mission that was both local and global. Spiritual dynamism could be measured accordingly!

Rocky was the road that brought the Early Church to the nations. In his commentary on Acts, mission strategist Peter Wagner paints in poignant terms the gut-wrenching dilemma that was Simon Peter's: Peter "was born again but he still behaved according to the rules that his mother and father had taught him. One thing Peter's mother had taught him was never to enter a Gentile house, and he probably had never previously violated this rule."[7] So when God directed Peter to visit the home of a Roman soldier, "it is hard for us today to understand just how revolting to Peter" this would be. What an earthshaking revelation it was for Peter to understand that "God does not show favoritism but accepts men from every nation" (Acts 10:34). Winning our neighbors to Christ and taking the gospel to the nations are of equal importance in the heart of God. Wagner speculates that God chose Peter and not Paul for this break-through because Peter was not called to focus on cross-cultural witnessing. Peter's calling remained centered in near-neighbor evangelism, but God wanted Peter's heart to beat in sync with His heart for all the peoples of the world, and thus God sent Peter on this short-term mission assignment.[8] Peter was to be a local pastor with a heart for the world!

The Bible ends with a vision of the target at which the church is to be aiming its life and energy. And that target is global: "Before me was a great multitude that no one could count, from *every nation, tribe, people and language*" (Rev. 7:9, emphasis added). In the very last chapter, we see a river of life, watering trees that produce leaves "for the healing of the *nations*" (v. 2, emphasis added). The balm of Gilead is to be made available to all peoples, not just storehoused in the lives of the already saved and satiated saints.

Throughout the Bible we run into a God whose saving love is pulsing out to all peoples, both near and far. None is to be left without a winning witness to His offer of redemption. And from the beginning of the Bible we learn that God's plan is to use all His people to deliver that offer. Some of His people are gifted and called to serve cross-culturally, some are called to serve in their own culture, but all are saved to be sent—all are commissioned to be part of the grand plan, whether by going in person, in prayer, or with their pocketbook. I want to believe that all who are deployed in their own culture can also have room in their heart for the extension of the gospel beyond it, while those assigned to cross-cultural ministry will also care and pray about those doing the job "at home."

Mission Mobilization: Specialization or Infiltration?

With tongue in cheek, I sometimes tell my congregation that I will not die happy until there is a mission connection in *every* home. I believe every Christian is called to care about and be some way involved in Christ's global enterprise, both nearby and far away. I pray that every home in my church will wrap its heart around something exciting that God is doing both in and beyond our community. I no longer believe the mission of Christ is reserved for a few, elite, mission zealots. I am working to infiltrate every ministry and every home with the biblical vision for the world and with an exciting connection to some part of that unfolding vision. The whole church for the whole world is my audacious quest!

My wife actually showed me the way. Long before she worked vocationally in children's ministry, she was determined to infiltrate the hearts of children with the heart of Jesus for the world. She wrote a graded mission curriculum and recruited a host of adults to teach it, getting a fun and unforgettable mission lesson into every class twice a year. Not only did the kids get it but so did the adults! She's written several plays for kids, including a poignant one for Christmas and a powerful one for Easter that bring out the global dimensions of these typically M & M holidays. And she wrote a hilarious, 30-minute melodrama that highlights the global drama of the whole Bible. Again, after performing and seeing these plays, both kids and adults walk away with a new view of the Word and of the world![9]

Our congregation has a children's mission team that prepares a quarterly mission lesson that is designed, over a year, to keep families up-to-date and connected to the major mission commitments of our church family. Every Lent and Advent we prepare daily devotional guides with child-level stories about what God is doing in our mission partnerships around the world. Our families are reading about, praying for, and giving to these Kingdom ventures. We raise considerable funds, but more importantly, we are raising up W/W disciples.

Our teens are deeply involved in the mission causes supported by our whole church and lead our church in several. They plan and host an annual, multigenerational house-building weekend in Mexico, and they kick off our Lenten mission focus with a 30-hour famine that raises their awareness of world hunger and raises money for the unreached nomadic people group our church has adopted in Ethiopia.[10]

When our mission team began to search for an unreached people group to adopt, I knew the effort must be empowered through prayer. Where would I find the prayer backing needed? I was asking the Lord this in worship one Sunday as our choir was singing a powerful anthem. They sit behind the pastors. The word came like a flash: "Look behind you." The choir? I spoke to our dedicated music minister, who gave me permission to present the need. After I explained God's heart for the nations and the need for prayer, one longtime choir member stuck up her hand and declared, "No one has ever asked us to do anything other than sing. And we can do more for the Lord than that!" They enthusiastically took up the challenge. When we chose a Muslim group in Ethiopia, the choir was more than interested, and several choir members have become key players in our unreached people-group team!

We do not put much energy into mission conferences. Instead, we take the mission of our church to our people's homes, Sunday classes, and worship services. We've streamlined mission team commissionings so that they are brief, tucked into the dedication of our morning offering, and followed up by a table on our patio where dozens of folks pick up a prayer itinerary for the team.

In the past 10 years our mission philosophy has grown along two lines. We used to send money to a host of ministries, with little personal connection to many. We were spread a mile wide and a millimeter deep (and boasted of all our missionaries and mission causes!). It came to us that this approach bred superficiality; we barely knew them, and they scarcely knew us. We now operate according to the mantra "narrow and deep." We ask what God wants us to contribute to His global kingdom enterprise, realizing that we can do only a few things well, and have settled on several long-term commitments. We have a much easier time declining to support the many wonderful ministries that do not fit into His foci for us.

The second line of growth that God has placed on our hearts is a strategy of Kingdom advance that centers on long-term global partnerships. We launched three major international commitments in the past five years—a Muslim tribe in Ethiopia, an impoverished village in Oaxaca, Mexico, and a missionary hospital in Kenya. Though ambitious in scope, we have seen our congregation joyfully embrace all three, with different saints attracted to each. We have brought into these partnerships key mission agencies whose expertise has been invaluable to us and to the extension of the gospel in these three places.

It is really an exciting new day in missions. Mission agencies are increasingly seeking local churches out, not as a source of funding for agency projects, but as full-fledged mission partners. In all three cases, we knew God's calling on us and sought out agencies that could help us fulfill that calling. We have also felt God leading us to share these thrilling partnerships with other congregations, so that we see ourselves as something of a catalyst congregation. The second congregation to sign on with our unreached people partnership is the smallest church in our presbytery. It is an elderly church without much money; but can they ever pray!

Long-term relationships are a telling witness to the character of Christ. I will never forget the second time we visited the remote Muslim group we "adopted." Muslim leaders exclaimed on several occasions: "You came back. We didn't think you would. Nobody else does." Long-term, multichurch, and agency partnerships also witness to the glorious unity of the global church. We partner with indigenous mission agencies in all three of our partnership settings and suspect the joyous fellowship we experience with our African and Latin sisters and brothers is both pleasing to our Father and a witness to our non-Christian friends in those places.

A few years ago my church's mission team challenged our elders to tithe the money we were raising for a building project on our campus. Using this money, we partnered with a Spirit-filled Kenyan church to build a maternity ward at their mission hospital. I wish you could have been in our congregation last Sunday when the head nurse of the maternity ward told us about the mighty works that Christ has already done at the recently completed ward. There was a hush of wonder and then a spontaneous eruption of applause and praise. I think our people felt immensely proud to be part of a church that was reaching out with the blessings of the gospel in such a concrete, life-uplifting way. It adds immeasurably to the spiritual dynamism that God is granting to our congregation these days.

To God be all the glory!

Notes

1. Philip Yancey, "Holy Sex," *Christianity Today*, vol. 47, No. 10, October 2003, 47.

2. I write about this more extensively in the book *Let My People Know . . . and Go* (Presbyterian Center for Mission Studies, 1996).

3. John Stott, "The Living God Is a Missionary God," *Perspectives on the World Christian Movement* (Pasadena, Calif.: William Carey Library, 1999), 4.

4. Walter Kaiser, "Israel's Missionary Call," *Perspectives*, 1999, 12.

5. Ibid.

6. Johannes Verkuyl, "The Biblical Foundation for the Worldwide Mission Mandate," *Perspectives*, 33.

7. Peter Wagner, *Acts of the Holy Spirit* (Regal Books, 2000), 228.

8. Ibid., 229.

9. These plays can be purchased from the Presbyterian Center for Mission Studies, 626-398-2468.

10. We partner with World Vision and use their 30-Hour Famine materials, supplementing them with information and inspiration about our own mission project.

For Further Reading

Duewel, Wesley L. *Touch the World Through Prayer*. Grand Rapids: Zondervan Publishing House, 1986.

Elliot, Elisabeth. *A Chance to Die: The Life and Legacy of Amy Carmichael*. Old Tappan, N.J.: Fleming H. Revell Company, 1987.

Guder, Darrell L., ed. *Missional Church*. Grand Rapids: William B. Eerdmans Publishing Company, 1998.

International Bulletin of Missionary Research. Quarterly journal published by the Overseas Ministries Study Center, Jonathon J. Bonk, ed., New Haven, Conn.

Johnstone, Patrick. *The Church Is Bigger than You Think*. Great Britain: Christian Focus Publishing, 1998.

———— and Jason Mandryk. *Operation World, 21st Century Edition*. Waynesboro, Ga.: Paternoster USA, 2001. (798 pages)

Mission Frontiers. Bimonthly journal published by the U.S. Center for World Mission, Ralph D. Winter, ed., Pasadena, Calif.

Newbegin, Leslie. *The Gospel in a Pluralistic Society*. Grand Rapids: William B. Eerdmans Publishing Company, 1989.

Olsen, Bruce. *Bruchko*. Orlando, Fla.: Creation House Books, 1993.

Perkins, John M. *Beyond Charity: The Call to Christian Community Development*. Grand Rapids: Baker Books, 1993.

Piper, John. *Let the Nations Be Glad! The Supremacy of God in Missions*. Grand Rapids: Baker Books, 1993.

Pirolo, Neal. *Serving as Senders*. San Dimas, Calif.: Emmaus Road, International, 1991.

Tucker, Ruth A. *From Jerusalem to Irian Jaya: A Biographical History of Christian Missions*. Grand Rapids: Zondervan Publishing House, 1983.

Winter, Ralph D., and Steven C. Hawthorne. *Perspectives on the World Christian Movement: A Reader*. Pasadena, Calif.: William Carey Library, 1999.